Praise

Walls of a Warrior

"One of the most important experiences readers of this book will encounter is **identifying** the walls that have been built around their hearts. Dawna states, "Identifying the walls we put in place is the first step to deconstructing them." You will be taken on a journey and gently come face-to-face with your walls, like 'Walls of Esteem', 'Walls of Masks', 'Walls of Isolation', and 'Walls of Resentment and Fear'. Through your travels, you will be guided step-by-step to identify, acknowledge, and tear down these unhealthy walls. In the chapter, 'Walls of Hurt', the author shares scientific facts that are both captivating and enlightening. You work toward a goal, building 'Healthy Walls' at the end of the book.

"*Walls of a Warrior* holds truth and encouragement that causes each reader to return to its insights again and again. A great read and phenomenal resource for personal healing and spiritual growth."

—Dr. Jean McLachlan Hess, Pastor of 316 Denver Church, Author, *Journey to the Manger,* Speaker

"At the end of the day, we are all human, with real feelings of fear. We are not alone in this journey called life. Dawna teaches us we cannot do life alone. She helps us reach out, break down walls, and live outside our comfort zones. *Walls of a Warrior,* speaks directly to women, whispers to men, and helps both to conquer their fears."

—Carmen Swick, Award-Winning Author for Children's Books—*Patch Land Adventures,* Speaker, and President of the Denver Chapter, Foundation Fighting Blindness

"Dawna knocks down walls and reveals our authentic core desires. Connection and safety are two of the most important human needs; our soul longs for authentic relationships. The human spirit thrives on positive, life-giving interpersonal connection with God and people. God created us to love and be loved, and to see and to be seen, in relationship with Himself and with others. We have all created walls in order to survive the storms in life; however, most of those walls no longer serve us. They actually hold us back from the fullness of connection, which Jesus desires to lead us into experiencing. Dawna guides the reader back to their God-given ability to show up with confidence and love in all their relationships. *Walls of a Warrior* is a must read, as it guides the reader back to their God-given natural state of being: a conqueror, peace filled, and loving human being capable of deep, life giving, connections."

—Lauren E Miller, Founder of Stress Solutions University.com, Speaker and Award-Winning, Best Selling Author

"With honesty, courage and eloquence, Dawna shares her calling to help others conquer their fears of the heart. In reading *Walls of a Warrior,* I am better equipped to answer the question, "Who am I?""

—Sam Adams, Comedian and Author of *If You Don't Believe Me . . . Lessons Learned From Listening to the Greats*

"Being a Jericho Girl lead me on a journey to wholeness. Not only did I recognize my walls through these pages, but Dawna gave me the tools to bring them to ruin. *Walls of a Warrior,* has helped me to emerge a warrior, and empowered me to live life with courage, and face the impossible."

—Gaye Taylor, Stonecroft Ministries Colorado Regional Speaker Trainer

WALLS

of a WARRIOR

Conquering the fears of our hearts

DAWNA HETZLER

DocUmeant *Publishing*
244 5th Avenue
Suite G-200
NY, NY 10001
646-233-4366
www.DocUmeantPublishing.com

DocUmeant Publishing
244 5th Avenue, Suite G-200
NY, NY 10001

Phone: 646-233-4366

Unless otherwise indicated, all Scripture quotations are taken from the HOLY BIBLE, NEW INTERNATIONAL VERSION®. NIV®. Copyright © 1973, 1978, 1984 by International Bible Society. Used by permission of Zondervan. All rights reserved worldwide.

Scripture quotations marked MSG are taken from THE MESSAGE. Copyright © by Eugene H. Peterson 1993, 1994, 1995, 1996, 2000, 2001, 2002. Used by permission of NavPress Publishing Group.

Scripture quotations marked (NLT) are taken from the Holy Bible, New Living Translation, copyright © 1996, 2004, 2007 by Tyndale House Foundation. Used by permission of Tyndale House Publishers, Inc., Carol Stream, Illinois 60188. All rights reserved.

Tool Box Note Cards designed by Carla Autrey, Artist

Cover Design and Layout by Ginger Marks
DocUmeant Designs

www.DocUmeantDesigns.com

This book may be purchased in bulk for educational, business, fund-raising, or sales promotional use. For information, please contact DocUmeant Publishing publisher@DocUmeantPublishing.com

ISBN13: 9781937801533
ISBN10: 1937801535

Printed in The United States of America

This book is dedicated to my grandmother, Neva Victoria Bonanno. You always called me Bella, your beautiful girl. I will forever keep your love and our memories close to my heart.

"Have I not commanded you? Be strong and courageous. Do not be afraid; do not be discouraged, for the LORD your God will be with you wherever you go" (Joshua 1:9).

CONTENTS

ACKNOWLEDGMENTS

I am indebted to a number of people who made this book possible. A special thanks to Kimberly Christian who helped lead discussions with the Jericho Girls and used her life experiences to help us all relate. Kimberly, listening to the still small voice of God, encouraged me to write this book.

To Tamera Stanley for her wise counsel and attentive spirit. You have led the Jericho Girls in amazing discussions and enriched our journey. Both of you lovelies took me to the next level of my faith.

To the Jericho Girls, who shared their hearts and some pretty tough life stories; you have facilitated bringing down the walls of my heart and I will be forever grateful.

To Ann Maloney, who opened her home for our meetings. Ann, your hospitality opened the doors of our hearts, allowing us to share in the intimacy of your home.

Thank you to Carol Keller for your profound wisdom and spiritual mentoring.

To Sally Smith, who was my "rear guard" and reminded me each day to write—"just keep writing." Thanks, Sally, for being my encourager.

To Anne Steinbroner, thank you for giving up the commodity of your time. Anne, you are gifted.

The truth is that all my sisters teach me, guide me, and call me out when needed. They have helped me grow in a mighty way. If I were to list them and thank each one individually, I would need to write another book. I cannot imagine life without you all.

To Larry Keller, for asking, "How can I help?" Larry, you are an amazing servant of God.

To Carla Autrey, God's beautiful artist. Thank you for creating the Jericho Girls' Tool Box Note Cards.

Carmen Swick and Lauren E Miller, thanks for your incredible, and much needed support.

To my high school friend, Jim Boling who shares my passion for teaching.

To my dad, mom, and sister who always encourage me to follow my dreams and to my mother-in-law, Caryl who dragged me to my first Bible study, thank you.

An eternal thank you to my husband David, who pushes and stretches me like no one can. You are my D.O.E. (Director of Everything). Thanks for letting me have my "30 clubs"—I love you!

FOREWORD

Jericho Girls is what we call ourselves—warrior women who work on breaking down our walls together. We met once a month for a year, and it was an incredible growth experience. God did amazing things in our group as His presence and strength was felt throughout our journey. We had a great leader, Dawna, whose passion and love for God came out in each step of the process. That process is what Dawna describes in the pages that follow.

For me, this journey was very valuable. After having a series of bad relationships, I was at a point in my life where I had given up on friendships and connecting with people. I was invited to a Bible study at Southeast Christian Church in Parker, Colorado, and decided to give it a try. I kept hearing God tell me that these women were for real, to open up to them, and to trust them. He knew that I had been hurt in the past, but this group would show me how to open my heart again. Dawna and I struck an immediate bond, and she was the warm and inviting support that I needed to feel comfortable starting a friendship again. Even though I had joined this Bible study and was getting to know some of the women there, I still felt this prompting from God to work harder at opening up.

Then Dawna shared that she was starting a new ministry, *The Walls of Jericho* to "work on walls that surround our hearts." She asked me if I would join the group in which the women became known as the "Jericho Girls". I felt like God was shouting, "YES!" and that this was exactly what He wanted me to do. However, I didn't jump in with both feet because I knew it would be difficult for me and somewhat scary. But I went and God worked on me in amazing ways. It turned out to be a small group and a safe place to share. I learned that when you talk through things with godly women, issues have less of a hold on you. I learned that not only do you need wonderful sisters in Christ to get their perspectives on situations, but that God also works through them to teach you things. I learned so much about myself on this journey. Our group has an amazing bond now, because we have supported each other through so many of life's circumstances.

I hope that you are blessed to find a group of women who want to work on their walls together. To have other women to discuss these in-depth topics that are covered in this book is a very important part of the process of addressing and tearing down the walls we have. It's also great to have others who will keep you focused and support you down the path that God leads you on. Having those encouragers that won't let us "give up because it's too hard" or being an encourager for someone else who is confiding in you is a blessing. The discussions, prayers, support, and love along the way are such a gift.

It was a privilege to be a part of this group, the process, and seeing Dawna's calling to work on her walls, turn into this amazing Jericho Girls group and then move into the book project. Dawna shares our journey to Jericho; and through reading *Walls of a Warrior*, you can now share in the experience that I had. The result is that God will help you get closer to your authentic self. Do you want to equip yourself to be the person God made you to be? Read on, my warrior friend—and enjoy the journey!

—Michelle Calhoun, one of the original Jericho Girls

INTRODUCTION

It all began with a Bible Study. Almost a decade ago, my mother-in-law, Caryl, invited me to a Women's Summer Bible study. I was so busy at the time with work, family life, and all the things in between that I told her I didn't have time to go. She proceeded to tell me that it was only once a week, for six weeks, and gently, but firmly, instructed me that I needed to be there. So I went, not quite kicking and screaming, but definitely complaining about how I still did not have time for an evening study.

I showed up and just listened. I drank in the Word of God and the fellowship of these lovely ladies. Who knew I needed this time? As I continued through the next six weeks, I was challenged to spend time alone studying my Bible. I remember actually speaking to God and saying, "Alright God, you want my time? You will get five minutes a day, and that is it!" Can you imagine speaking to God in such a way? But, He put up with me; and what I found was that the five minute commitment turned into ten. Then ten turned into twenty.

Looking back, I cannot discern exactly how my time increments transformed to longer spans, but at one point I realized I was spending about an hour with God each morning. It seemed like only five minutes, and I found myself wanting to stay even longer. Daily duties called, but I just wanted to be at the feet of Jesus.

I cannot emphasize enough how this time with Him transformed me. The women in my study group aided in my transformation too. I was having a love affair with Jesus and HIS ladies, and I was taken in by it all. Needless to say, I continued with the "Bible girls" week after week, month after month, and soon those months turned into years. Throughout the years, God allowed me to be used within the group. Yes, little ol' me—the one who showed up reluctantly with nothing to give. Now God was using me little by little—He is sneaky that way! What started as a six-week commitment turned into an incredible relationship with God and deep bonds with the women I would spend my Tuesday nights with.

This gave way to my next calling: a burning desire to help the less fortunate. God placed a desire in my heart to feed and share with the homeless. Many of the ladies joined me in a homeless ministry where we would serve breakfast once a month. But, my goal was to feed their souls, and not just their stomachs. Through Open Doors Ministries, we served breakfast, then sat and talked with "our friends on Colfax." We listened attentively to their heart wrenching stories. This continued for two years. I initially thought we would be a blessing to the homeless, and I am sure we were on some level. But what really happened was that they helped each of us who served, more than we could have ever blessed them.

Then, God placed on my heart a need for feeding the souls of ladies within our own group. I had a luncheon with two of my friends and we discussed what the ladies' needs were. We talked about starting a new ministry where we would choose one woman to minister and pray for. We discussed going to her home and bringing her food, gift cards, and just spending quality time together.

As we continued, we discovered there were many drawbacks to this particular type of ministry. We mulled over how we might choose one woman per month. By necessity, or . . . ? What if the women didn't want us to come to their homes? Was this too invasive? Some women felt more comfortable and closer to some than to others. Many women had a hard time asking for help. Out of this, a new question arose. "Why is it that we as women have a hard time asking for help?" One of my friends blurted out, "Because we all have walls!"

Why did her statement strike a chord within me? I felt an urgent desire to help our group break down the walls we had erected in our relationships. My friend had identified the crux of the matter. We have walls, and walls hinder our relationships. We began to discuss a women's ministry that would address our "walls." After much prayer, I felt a peace about beginning this new outreach. I had no idea that the need would be so great for others—and especially for me. Thus *The Walls of Jericho* was formed, and the women became known as "Jericho Girls". Our mission: To knock down the walls which hold our hearts hostage.

Before our first meeting, I sent an email invitation to the ladies within our Bible study group and to many of my friends who were not in the group. One of my friends wrote me back and said, "Thanks for the invite but I have been working on my walls and all of them have come down!"

I began to wonder if that was possible, or even healthy? Can all your walls really come down once and for all, and you never have to worry about them ever again? This is how our Jericho journey began. I invite you to travel with us on the road to Jericho, to explore the inner depths of your own heart, and to tear down the walls that surround your heart—brick-by-brick and stone-by-stone.

Every one of us has walls to deal with. As God helps you dismantle your walls, understand that we each progress at our own pace and in different ways. There is no formula for breaking down walls except for God's formula. Take your time. Re-read chapters before proceeding to the next if you feel stuck at any level. Know that you are not alone in your journey.

As we journey to Jericho together, it is my hope that the words and experiences of the Jericho Girls will help to transform you into the woman of God you were called to be—one without walls. I will be praying for you as you take this journey with us.

1

WHAT WALLS?

It was a hot summer day when I was invited to Hudson Gardens in Littleton, Colorado for a day of contemplation—the invitation was to an event called *Breathe*. I thought to myself, how wonderful that sounds—a few hours to escape the busyness of my hectic life. The invitation called to me "Come, find a spot alone in the gardens, and simply chat with God."

My mind raced with things I had to do that day. A real estate transaction was first on my "to do" list, and it would take priority over God for certain. It was 9 p.m. the night before the *Breathe* meeting and I had just gotten off the phone with a client. I had a conference call scheduled at 9 a.m. the next morning with him and then realized that was the same time I had an appointment with God to chat in the gardens. "Well," I thought, "maybe next time. Besides, who has time to breathe anyway?" I woke up the next morning and began to read my daily devotional for the day. It said, "Come away today from the worries of this life and find a solitary path to meet me." Immediately my mind jumped to the invitation to find God alone in the garden. "How can I make this happen, God?" I asked. Silence. It seemed as if He was disappointed that I would chose something, anything, over a Divine appointment with Him. I had to go. But how would my day handle itself without me on my conference call and juggling all the things I do before noon? THEN, He whispered to my heart, "Do you trust me?" "I do," I whispered back. Next thing I knew, I was in my car and headed to the lush garden escape—phone in one hand making my 9 a.m. phone call earlier than planned. I arrived at the peaceful garden, giving instructions on how to close the deal. My surroundings were peaceful but my heart raced as I tried to convey all the instructions needed to get the deal handled and move on to my anticipated "quiet time". As I hung up the phone, I felt like everything was, for the time being, under control.

I began to take in the beautiful surroundings. The facilitator instructed everyone to walk through the garden and expect to meet God. She instructed us to think of Eve walking through the garden, looking for God. I did as I was instructed and as I wandered through the garden, I came upon an incredible wetland area with the largest lily pads I have ever seen. Then I spotted it, a park bench hidden within the lush landscape. I sat. For the first time in a long time, I just listened. Usually, I spend my quiet time talking to God, but not that day. That day I was drained and just wanted to be with Him. It was then that He began to show me some things I needed to work on. I didn't realize it then, but He was doing some reconstructing and remodeling, and I was oblivious to it.

So there I was. Alone. At Hudson Gardens with God—peaceful, serene, my worries forgotten for the moment. Then I read the scripture:

> *Are you tired? Worn out? Burned out on religion? Come to me. Get away with me and you'll recover your life. I'll show you how to take a real rest. Walk with me and work with me—watch how I do it. Learn the unforced rhythms of grace. I won't lay anything heavy or ill-fitting on you. Keep company with me and you'll learn to live freely and lightly* (Matthew 11:29, MSG).

I was tired and worn out. I wanted a real rest. God's Word said, "Walk and work with me." I realized I had been spending my mornings with Him, but left Him at my "morning time" place as I headed off to work each day. Was that why I was burned out? I wasn't watching how *He was doing it.* I re-read the scripture out loud and kept revisiting the line, "learn the unforced rhythms of grace." What were these "unforced rhythms of grace" and how was I supposed to obtain them? Was I forcing rhythms? "What is it, God?" Impatiently I sat waiting for His answer. I read the scripture again, "I won't lay anything heavy or ill-fitting on you."

Then it happened . . . my mind began to wander. I started thinking about my favorite little lunch hang out, eating on the patio and watching the activity around me. A woman with her dog sat at the table across from me while she pecked away on her computer; a tattooed dad with his two children playing and laughing together. Just then, something caught my attention. A blind man walked by with his walking stick in one hand and his cell phone in the other. He chatted away with someone on the phone.

I watched in amazement how he navigated the patio table and chairs so gracefully, stopping from time to time to re-route his way. I chuckled to myself. I thought, *how funny is that?* If I were blind, that would be me—multitasking, chatting, and navigating all the while. I wondered if he had always been blind, or if he had sight and then lost it. These questions would remain unanswered. He did not seem to care that he was blind, or did he just begrudgingly accept his fate?

The stranger continued on until he was out of sight. My mind jumped back to where I *really was*—oh yes, Hudson Gardens. I began to ponder if, in some ways, was I "blinded" too? Was I navigating through life without "seeing"? I knew I was burned out and tired, but was I *blind?*

As if in answer, a gentle whisper, as if a voice on the breeze, spoke to me, "You are blinded to the fact that you have walls." "Who me?" I answered. "I don't have walls, God." (I love to argue, it must be my Italian heritage.) "This 'walls' thing isn't about me," I argued, "it is about the ladies we are going to minister to." At this point, I was glad to be alone because anyone watching would have thought I was cuckoo talking with my 'invisible friend'. Then more silence.

My time at Hudson Gardens was almost over. I had to meet with the ladies for lunch and then head back to finish out my work day. I was perturbed that God had the audacity to talk about *me* having walls.

I didn't realize it at the moment, but that day I had packed my bags and stepped onto a path that would take me to a far off land. As I began my trek, I realized I was headed on a journey to Jericho. Once there, I would need to march, yell, and knock over some pretty tall walls that surrounded the city of my heart. What I would soon discover is that I, too, had walls. Walls with God and walls with others, and that day I began my Journey to Jericho.

TYPES OF WALLS

My husband is a home builder. In building a new home, he creates walls. When he remodels a home, he typically knocks down walls. In the same way as he creates and knocks down, we do the same, constructing and deconstructing of the walls around our hearts. So what causes these walls to be put up in the first place? Conditioning, rejection, hurts, fears, being someone we are not—the list goes on and on. God informed me that I have walls. I didn't believe Him, or maybe I would not allow myself to believe that I could have walls. I thought I was pretty open with others and it was difficult for me to see that I had any walls at all. Maybe my friend, who wrote me the email that all her walls had come down, was in the same boat as I was—oblivious. So I began to think about what types of walls could possibly exist.

First, since I had not acknowledged that I have walls, there must be "invisible walls", walls that I do not allow myself to consciously think about. Geri Scazzero says in her book, *I Quit*, that:

> *You spiral downward by negatively interpreting the behavior of another and making assumptions about what they are thinking. These turn into hidden landmines in relationships. Slowly you build up walls of resentment. You hurt yourself. You build invisible walls to keep others out. And worst of all, you quench God's Spirit within you.*

Had I done this? Had I created landmines in my relationships and within myself? How can one build invisible walls and trick the mind into not acknowledging those walls are even there? Well, I must have, since God said it was so.

Next, I asked my husband about the types of walls he deals with in his business. He informed me that although there are many different types, the two most important walls are structural and non-structural walls.

He defined a structural wall as one that bears weight, one that can maintain, uphold and keep the integrity of the structure. I thought this is a good wall to have, a healthy wall. We need to have healthy walls in place to keep the integrity of the heart intact. Therefore this type of wall, a healthy structural wall, should be in place.

He also told me about non-structural walls. They do not bear structural weight and are used to divide and separate. These are the walls around our hearts that create barriers within ourselves, with others, and most seriously, with God. These are the types of walls that need to come down.

We also discussed floating walls: they are built to be attached at the top and are not attached at the bottom allowing the wall to move with expansive soils. I found this type of wall most interesting. Walls we allow to float, peering over and then ducking back down. Tearing down and building back up. I related these types of walls as putting on a "mask" and taking it off again. This is yet another type of wall around my heart that needs to come down.

Fire walls are another interesting type of wall. They are made to protect from fire or other extremes. Not having the wrong kinds of walls but building balanced, healthy walls seems to be the key. My husband shared with me about many types of walls, but these were the ones I wanted to begin searching my heart for. More than that was simply too overwhelming. So who did I have walls with? Could I have walls with God, and if so, what would they be? I would soon find out. . . .

WALLS WITH GOD

As I began praying and asking God about my walls, I was led to the scripture in Joshua 6. Here, God instructs Joshua and his fighting men, with seven priests blowing trumpets and carrying the Ark of the Covenant, to march around the city walls daily for six days in silence. But the seventh day was different. Joshua was instructed to have his group march around the city seven times, with the priest blowing their ram's horn trumpets. On the seventh time around, when the priest sounded a long blast on their trumpet, the people were to shout and the walls of Jericho would collapse—and they did!

Huh, I thought. If we are to obey God's commands and shout, the walls can come down. So I followed God's command to pursue my walls and to march around the city walls of my heart.

The *Jericho Girls* began to meet to discuss what walls we had. It was a slow and difficult journey as we began to share what types of walls we have and what we could do to dismantle them. As we journeyed together and started to "shout" (discussing our walls), our walls began to come crumbling down. Our first meeting led us on a discussion of, "what walls do I have?" What walls do I have with God and with others? It was an interesting discussion, and once we were given the ability to verbalize our walls, we were awakened to the fact that many of us have walls with God.

Together, we began to learn that the walls we have with others are the same walls we put in place to keep God at bay. Interestingly, we tend to project our earthly relationships onto God, attributing to Him human weaknesses and foibles. However, our earthly relationships should not and cannot depict a true concept of God. For example, maybe you never had a father growing up. In response to never knowing your father, you believe that God is absent in your life, too. Or maybe your father was a harsh, dictatorial type. In that instance, you might grow up believing that God is judgmental and waiting to punish you when you violate his rules.

On the flip side, we can be in a relationship where the person oozes the love of God and we get a glimpse of Jesus; however, we never get a full picture of God based on human interactions. The only way to understand who God *truly* is, is to peer into the Word of God, spend time with Him, and cultivate relationships with other believers.

Getting real with God seems to be the first step in attacking our walls. We tend to hide behind masks and pretend we are something we are not before God. I am not sure why we do this since He knows everything about us—but we do nonetheless. Somewhere along our journey, we find ourselves skirting through life, pretending all is right with God. This denial enables us to deflect the real issues that need to be brought to light. God knows those issues and He can help us through them, but we often won't let Him. When we try to hide our "baggage" from God (even though He can see it anyway), we bury those issues deep inside our hearts. This is when we lay the foundation for the walls that inhibit God and others from seeing the true person we are. It may seem safe to do this rather than confronting and dealing with what is really going on in our lives. But in reality, we are creating walls so thick that, with time, no one will recognize who we are.

WALL OF SHAME

A huge wall we tend to construct is the wall of shame. This is not the same as the hall of fame. Wikipedia defines the Wall of Shame as

> *Originally a term used by western politicians and media to refer to the Berlin Wall, and more generally a negative term for a separation barrier that, in the opinion of those using the term, brings shame upon the builders or others. In some cases, it is the circumstances of the wall's construction or its intended purpose that is fingered as bringing dishonor.*

Typically when we make mistakes or life has dealt us a life situation we are not proud of, we tend to hide. We don't want others to see our failures and we certainly don't want God to see them. The natural tendency is to hide or run instead of return. But what keeps us on the run versus turning and running quickly back to God? Mostly, I believe it's because we, as humans, tend to gravitate toward sin.

I have a Siberian Husky that loves to chase rabbits. However, she can be in mid-flight chasing a rabbit and all I have to say is, "Hanah, come girl." She turns on a dime and returns to me. This is highly atypical for a Husky! But what Hanah has learned is that she gets lots of love (and treats) when she obeys my command. However, Hanah had to learn this through experience. When I first rescued her, she roamed free on our 35 acre home site. She had to be trained to "come" on command. One day during her training period, she saw something move out of the corner of her eye. Ah! Something to chase. I called to her and said, "Hanah stay." As I got within reaching distance to her, she took off after the mystery creature. Next I heard a big YELP! Yep, she had done it; she had met the neighborhood porcupine.

For the next thirty minutes, she heard my voice scolding her all the way to the vet, "When I say come, you come! When I say stay, you stay. See, you stupid dog, you should have listened to me." She looked ashamed of what she had done aside from being in a lot of pain—poor little pup. She just wanted to hide her face from me; she knew she should have listened.

Isn't it the same way with God? We disobey and we run away from Him rather than towards Him. We forget He is quick to forgive us and take us back. The difference is that God doesn't shame us or tell us, "I told you so." He opens His loving arms and says, *"Return child."* When we don't return to Him, we end up living in shame and away from Him. Yet, all He wants is for us to return to the safety of His arms.

Ever since that incident, Hanah has always obeyed my voice. Somehow she understands that I have her best interest at heart. Not all of us learn to return to God after one encounter with the "porcupines" of our lives. Maybe dogs are smarter than us. Unfortunately for some of us, it will take many encounters with the porcupines in our lives before we began to obey and listen the first time and return when called. I strive to have a heart like Hanah.

WALL OF FEAR

So now for the real issue… I was at a point where I had to address my biggest wall with God. It was a wall of fear. Fear that God would ask something of me that I am not ready for or maybe never ready to do. Fear of being scolded and shamed rather than accepted and loved. I know that He truly doesn't operate this way, but sometimes I allow my fear to override what I truly know about God and it is tempting to stay away. There have been times when I didn't want to face my issues. If I address fears with God, won't He require me to face them? I knew the answer was yes, but was I ready to face them? So, as I began to dismantle my wall of fear with God, I started quoting scriptures about fear.

Be strong and courageous. Do not be afraid or terrified because of them, for the LORD your God goes with you; he will never leave you nor forsake you (Deuteronomy 31:6).

For God did not give us a spirit of timidity, but a spirit of power, of love and of self-discipline (2 Timothy 1:7).

The LORD is my light and my salvation—

> *whom shall I fear?*

The LORD is the stronghold of my life—

> *of whom shall I be afraid?* (Psalm 27:1).

I began improving my relationship with Him and spending time addressing my concerns and my fears. <u>What did I find? I found that my fears were false.</u> God will never ask me to do something that is beyond my capability, maybe out of my comfort zone, but nothing I am not already equipped to do. He will not shame me; rather He always welcomes me back with open arms. What I found was that as I dismantled my wall of fear before him, I was safe. My heart has been transformed by the One whose character is Love. I still find myself on the run and fearful from time to time, but what I find now is that I return quicker than before. For that, I am forever working towards developing a heart like my little Siberian Husky, Hanah. A heart that stops me from reconstructing the wall which holds me away from Him.

WALLS WITH OTHERS

It is natural to have walls with others. You cannot let someone in without first beginning a relationship with that person. A relationship develops, trust begins to build and when you feel ready (and everyone feels ready at different times) you begin to share your hopes and dreams, stories and journeys with that person. Whether it's a friend or someone you are looking to date, it is the same pattern: get to know, trust, and share.

As we get to share and open up in a relationship, we become vulnerable. There is a risk involved at this point. One has to evaluate, that is, ask the question *"is it worth the risk"* and weigh the benefits versus the risk of sharing. Each one of us carries our own life experience from childhood that enables us to either share or hold back. Some of us have been hurt more than others. Some of us are scarred for life. So we have to discern if this is a person that is worthy of our heart. Some people are not.

A dear friend, who had many hurtful relationships in her life, was struggling at one point in our relationship to open her heart to me. She held her hand outward as if to stop me from coming any closer and she said, "When I first met you, you were here, at a distance from me. Now, in our friendship, you are here." She then moved her arm in half way closer to her body. I had gotten fifty percent closer to her than when I first started to hang out with her. This was about one year into our friendship. She needed time to see who I was. Was I for real? Was I going to hurt her somehow? She began to realize that I wasn't going to hurt her. Later on in our friendship as she allowed me in closer, I told her that I could potentially hurt her. Not intentionally, of course, but I am human and I make mistakes.

We agreed that if I ever did something to hurt or offend her, she would come to me to talk about it. We would work hard together to maintain a friendship with the best possible trust level one can humanly do. Over the years, we have become like sisters. She has seen my highs and she has seen my lows. I am not certain if she will ever totally deconstruct her wall with me. It is my belief that she allows one brick to remain in front of her heart. But it is only one brick. Maybe that brick will always be in place, but that is alright. I see how far she has come, letting her guard down, how she has grown, how our relationship has blossomed, and I love what I see.

It is not an easy task, letting down your guard. It has been a journey for me too. My wall with others is not a trust issue. Mine revolves more around being needed too much. I tend to take on a lot. When I take on too much, I continue to juggle it all until I am exhausted. I tend to build walls around my heart so that others don't see that truly, I cannot do it all. Before I dealt with this wall, if someone was too needy, I would push them way. I would evaluate if this person was going to take too much of my time and energy. If I thought they would, I tended toward pushing away. I was able to bring down this wall by setting limits with others and myself. I still take on too much, but I am implementing more realistic limits and saying no when I need to. This allows me to build friendships rather than pushing them away.

What walls do you have with others? What is it that is hindering you from having true friendships that allow others to experience life with you? Identifying the walls that we put in place is the first step in deconstructing them.

A few things we can do to identify our walls: First, go to a trust friend or mentor and ask what they see in you that hinders your relationships. Next, take those things to God and ask Him how He would have you deal with them. Finally, spend some time in self-examination. Many times we know the issues that we have. We simply don't want to see them because change is difficult. We need to identify our walls—name them. Making a list is a good way to start. Can you identify them and understand why they are in place?

Jericho Girls' Response: Can you identify with them?

- *I never fully acknowledged that I have walls.*
- *I am tired of being afraid. It is time for me to deal with my walls.*
- *I have walls I don't consciously acknowledge.*
- *Walls are built one brick at a time—in layers like an onion.*
- *We can't change what we don't acknowledge.*

Jericho Girls' Tool Box

At our first meeting, one of the Jericho Girls said that we need tools to accomplish our goals. As a result, I began creating a "tool box" for each of us. Each meeting I would hand out a note card with a scripture to memorize so that we would have the tools we need to call upon as we deconstruct our walls.

Put on your *safety goggles* so your vision is not compromised.

"See, I have engraved you on the palms of my hands; your walls are ever before me" (Isaiah 49:16).

TRAINING YOUR SOUL AND BREAKING DOWN WALLS:

Putting things into practice: I found that having spiritual practices in my life helps me grow and stretch. At the end of each chapter, you will find training for your soul that will help you apply what you have learned.

Lectio Divina *(Latin for divine reading)*

Traditionally, Lectio Divina has four separate steps: *read, meditate, pray, and contemplate.* First a passage of Scripture is read, and then its meaning is reflected upon. This is followed by prayer and contemplation on the Word of God.

Slowly read Joshua 6 practicing Lectio Divina. Note what words or verses really stick with you. Once you have some words or verses that really resonate with you, re-read them slowly and meditate on them. Pray about what is on your heart after reading these words or verses. Read them not as text, but rather as a love letter from God. Contemplate what God is saying to you.

2
WHO AM I?

TELL ME AGAIN WHO I AM

Generally speaking, most women cannot identify who they are. When asked the question of *who am I*, the natural response is, I am a wife, a daughter, a sister, a business woman, an entrepreneur. But is that *who I truly am?* What if those labels were stripped from me? Who would I be then? As these questions began to well up, I pondered on the fact that these titles shape how I perceive myself (or how others perceive me), but they are not who I *really* am. We tend to get so wrapped up in our identities that we eventually begin to forget who we really are. The memory of who we truly are eventually fades. We can become "dead" to who we really are. I witnessed first-hand what happens when your so-called identity is stripped. My husband is a home builder, and in 2008 the real estate market nationwide took a strong downturn. He was building high-end homes in Colorado where we live. Suddenly, for the first time since high school, he was out of work and was faced with the same question. Without work for three long years, he was constantly asking, "If I am not a home builder, then who am I?" He had so identified himself as a successful home builder that when his work was no longer, he could not figure out who he was. Success as a home builder was all he knew.

Remember the blind guy navigating his way through the outdoor restaurant? I was having lunch when I noticed the man maneuvering through the tightly placed patio tables. He did this so elegantly— guiding himself with his "seeing eye stick" in one hand and holding his cell phone up to his ear with the other. I was so taken in by the sight of this marvelous man that I smiled as he wandered through the tables and chairs, while he was laughing with the person on the phone. While studying him, I began to think, what if I were born blind? What if I had never been able to see a sunset or the breathtaking beauty of the Colorado mountains or to behold the night sky and catch my breath when I saw a falling star? What if I had no way to identify who I am through my reflection? To never see my features and to judge them whether good or bad? At that point, I was overwhelmed with thankfulness that I had the privilege of such a gift. The gift of eyesight. Even though many a time I had taken this for granted, that day was different. I began to see things in a new light.

As I sat pondering, I began to imagine myself as blind. No external input, just darkness. I sat in the sun with my eyes closed but I could still see some light. I wondered, does a blind person ever see any hint of light, or is it pure darkness? Obviously it depends on their condition, but one can wonder.

I thought about who I was on the inside without any external influence. I whispered my descriptions out loud. "I am serious. I am silly. I love nature. I am an extrovert who truly loves when I can be an introvert"—in other words, I love my alone time. "Even though I believe I can do it all, I really can't. I need others. I am an encourager, but I need encouragement. I am an animal lover. Except for snakes— I hate snakes!" Could a fear of snakes be yet another one of my walls? Could it be a wall of fear or, maybe deeper yet, a fear of being deceived? Hmmm, something to add to my list of walls to work on. "I am funny. I am flirtatious." I am more than the superficial labels that do not reveal what I do, what I believe, or who I am to others. I am a child of God who has been hard-wired with many unique inner features. These are the things that determine who I really am. The external things add to who I am, but they do not completely define me.

Many women identify who we are with what we do. We are daughters, wives, mothers, working professionals and so on. When I posed the question to the Jericho Girls, the typical responses were expressed: I am a mother, a wife, a business professional—all expected answers. The deeper question was, who am I REALLY? How has God hard-wired you? What makes you tick? What are the inner desires of your heart? The truth of the matter was that many of us did not have an answer. We truly didn't know who we were. We get so wrapped up in our lives and living our roles as mother, wife, and working professional that when we stop to ponder the question, we truly do not know. How can this be? At what point do we stop being who we are as the result of morphing into our typical roles? It is a subtle shift, and I don't believe that we even notice that it is happening. Before we know it, we wake up with a blurred vision of our lives not able to clearly identify who we are on the inside.

Sometimes we don't identify or, appreciate how God has hard-wired us as a good thing or a gift. For example, I have always seen myself as being serious, and that is not a trait I particularly like. I would much rather be funny than serious. I like to make others smile and laugh. Why would God give me a gift of seriousness? He obviously has a reason. Once I began to identify it as a gift, I began to see myself in a different light. When I acknowledged that my identity was created by God and each trait was God's original design for my life, I began to love those things I once thought were not so special. "I praise you because I am fearfully and wonderfully made; your works are wonderful, I know that full well" (Psalm 139: 14).

As women, we tend to be very hard on ourselves. We need to cherish how God has uniquely made us. Do you believe you are *fearfully and wonderfully made*? Do you believe that God's *works are wonderful*? Do you know that full well?

Geri Scazzero says in her book, *I Quit!*, "There is no one else in the world like you. No one! One of the greatest ways to honor and glorify God is through embracing your unrepeatable life."

Stop wanting to be someone else and embrace the true you. Once you can identify who you *really* are, you can embrace who God has made you. Then you will begin to love who you *really* are, and then you can love others well—without walls. You have an unrepeatable life, now love it!

My Friends Tell Me Who I Am

"Friends help each other understand who they are. They define one another over the course of a lifetime." Michael Card, *A Fragile Stone.*

In 1985, I went on a date with a guy who would eventually become my husband. On our first date, we went to see the movie, *The Breakfast Club.* Not too long ago, we watched it again as a rerun on television. I still enjoyed it just as much as the first time I saw it with him over twenty-eight years ago. The story depicted five characters, the princess, the basket case, the athlete, the brain, and the criminal. Each of them, spending their weekend in high school detention. At the beginning of their detention day, they all just wanted to get through the day; and it appeared they had nothing in common nor did they seem to care to know one another. As discussions continued throughout the day, they began to share about themselves little-by-little. They discovered that even though they had very different backgrounds, they were actually very similar. They began sharing their stories (our stories are powerful), and as they did, they found connection and healing in sharing. Here is the letter that was written by "the brain" at the end of their detention day:

Brian Johnson (the Brain):

Dear Mr. Vernon, we accept the fact that we had to sacrifice a whole Saturday in detention for whatever it was we did wrong. What we did WAS wrong, but we think you're crazy to make us write an essay telling you who we think we are. You see us as you want to see us... in the simplest terms and the most convenient definitions. But what we found out is that each one of us is ... a brain...

Andrew Clark: ...and an athlete...

Allison Reynolds: ...and a basket case...

Claire Standish: ...a princess...

John Bender: ...and a criminal...

Does that answer your question?

Sincerely yours, the Breakfast Club.

The movie teaches us many valuable lessons. First, sharing and being heard promotes healing. Second, don't be too quick to judge others. Everyone has a story that leads them to where they are in life. When explored, one might recognize that their story is strikingly similar to another's. Sometimes, we are surprisingly like others, even though we may not initially appear to be. Third, others help point us to who we truly are.

One of the most valuable tools I found in learning who I am has been discussions and interactions with my friends. I have a very special friend I call Buddy. I have known her since I was fifteen years old. We were kids when we first met. We have gone through a lot together. In fact, we didn't even like each other at first. We were both receptionists at a real estate office. I thought she was nothing like me. She dressed and spoke differently. For some reason, I just didn't like her, and she felt the same about me. But something happened. I am not sure when, but at some point in our working relationship we began to get to know each other. Our external appearances and behaviors seemed to fade as a friendship began to develop. I think about the blind guy. . . . What if I were blind when I met Buddy? Would our hearts have connected immediately since I would not have been able to judge her by external factors?

Almost thirty years later, we have developed a very special friendship. We have seen a lot of change in each other throughout those years. We started out in the same direction, then went in different directions, then headed back in the same direction again. She knows everything about me, and we have experienced life together. We live in different states now, but our hearts are still close. As I reflect on our deep friendship, I realize that she has defined who I am and who I am *not*. Every time I talk with her on the phone, we still giggle like the young girls we once were. She brings out my silliness, my playful side, and she makes me smile and laugh.

We reminisce about fun little things we did when we were first getting to know each other. She speaks plain truth to me, and we discuss the intimate details of our lives with unfiltered words. Her words bring me back to reality. We discuss where we are failing in life so honestly and openly that sometimes I cannot decipher if I am talking with her or the inner depths of myself. In those discussions of our failings, it reminds me of who I am not.

She is the only person I have ever shared this type of friendship with—one with whom I have no walls and no reservations about speaking from my open heart. She has never judged me and has always been there for me. Michael Card, in his book, *A Fragile Stone*, says; "It has been my experience that friends define each other. When I am uncertain about the direction in my life, I go to my closest friends to affirm, or perhaps reaffirm, who I am and what the calling on my life is all about." Buddy does that for me. She affirms and sometimes reaffirms who I am, which helps define who I truly am. She also helps me see who I am not. When I am headed on the wrong path, she points it out to me. Sometimes directly, sometimes indirectly. She helps me see that heading in a wrong direction is not me, neither who I am nor where I belong. She is my compass, pointing me back in the direction I should go. I hope everyone can have a "Buddy" like mine in their life.

THE SCRIPTURES TELL ME WHO I AM

When we look to the Bible, we see many stories of God affirming who a person is. In the story of Jesus and the woman at the well (John 4:1–42), Jesus tells her she is someone who wants more than her current life. He tells her that she thirsts for everlasting water. He tells her she is craving spiritual things.

When Jesus encounters the woman caught in adultery (John 8:1–11) and tells her she is forgiven, He admonishes her to "go and sin no more." In essence He is saying, "You are more than this. Go and do better. I know your heart, and this is not who you are."

Jesus calls Simon Peter (Matthew 16:18), "the rock" that He will build His church on. Despite all of Peter's failings, lack of faith, and denials, He tells Peter that he is more than his shortcomings. More than that, despite Peter's failures, Jesus will use him to build His church.

If we search, we can find many Bible stories showing God defining who we are and pointing us to our purpose. Specific scriptures can also point us to who we are in Christ. Memorize some of these and write them on your heart.

I Am Accepted

John 1:12: I am God's child;

John 15:15: As a disciple, and I am a friend of Christ;

Romans 5:1: I have been justified;

Colossians 2:9–10: I am complete in Christ;

I Corinthians 6:19–20: I have been bought with a price and I belong to God.

I Am Secure

Romans 8:1–2: I am free from condemnation;

Romans 8:28: I am assured that God works for my good in all circumstances;

2 Corinthians 1:21–22: I have been established, anointed and sealed by God;

Philippians 1:6: I am confident that God will complete the good work He has started in me;

2 Timothy 1:7: I have not been given a spirit of fear but of power, love and sound mind.

I Am Significant

John 15:16: I have been chosen and appointed to bear fruit;

Ephesians 2:10: I am God's workmanship;

Ephesians 3:12: I may approach God with freedom and confidence;

1 Corinthians 3:16: I am God's temple;

Philippians 4:13: I can do all things through Christ, who strengthens me.

This is just the beginning of what God says about His beloved children. Search the scriptures. Go on a treasure hunt for what God has to say about you. God has an incomprehensible love for you. His word reveals that you are fully forgiven, never forsaken, loved and cherished. He calls you His daughter, and so much more. Do you know that God delights in you and sings over you?

The LORD your God is with you, the Mighty Warrior who saves. He will take great delight in you; He will quiet you with his love, He will rejoice over you with singing (Zephaniah 3:17).

It is imperative to see yourself as God sees you. Understand that God is crazy in love with you and that He delights in you. This is foundational in understanding who you *truly* are and that it is safe to deconstruct your walls before Him.

Geoff Suratt said in a sermon at Southeast Christian church, "Purpose is God's plan for my life." We get wrapped up in the purpose of our jobs, our home lives, and with others. Those things consume so much of us that we forget our real purpose in life. All those are good things, but who we are wired to be, the details encoded in our DNA, is our purpose for God—how He has crafted and created us to be used for Him. *That* is our purpose and who we *truly are.* Until we discover that, our lives are lived out by things that define us, as things we do rather than who we are. We know this to be true because we all have an inner desire for more. We can have the best job, love being a mother and wife, we can have activities we enjoy, and still long for more. This longing occurs when we are not in tune with who God has called us to be and using His gifts in our lives. The more I know Christ, the more I can truly know who I am.

Ruth Haley Barton, in *Sacred Rhythms,* says,

> *Your desire for more of God than you have right now, your longing for love, your need for deeper levels of spiritual transformation than you have experienced so far is the truest thing about you. You might think that your woundedness or your sinfulness is the truest thing about you or that your giftedness or your*

personality type or your job title or your identity as husband or wife, mother or father, somehow defines you. But in reality, it is your desire for God and your capacity to reach for more of God than you have right now that is the deepest essence of who you are.

Knowing God and living out our unique God-ordained purpose is the main calling for our lives and defines who we truly are. Using our spiritual gifts in our daily lives gives us completeness and wholeness, and fills our lives with purpose. For example, my career as a real estate broker has become so entwined with who I am, an encourager and a confidant, that I am able to use my gifts while in my work setting.

Do you really know who God has created you to be? I am a woman of God who has been called to encourage others. I am crafted and created for a balanced life of interaction with others and well-planned alone time. God has blessed me with a husband to serve and share my life. God has hand-picked my career as a real estate broker to share the love of home ownership with others while ministering, guiding, and directing. God has intertwined my gifts with the things that complement what I do. But most of all, He has called me to Him. To know Him more deeply each day and as I work this dance of Love and weave it into the fibers of my day. In the work place, at home, with my friends, and in all that I do, I find the bona fide, unique calling for my life. Knowing *whose* I am and who I have been hand-crafted to be reveals to me who I truly am. When I understand who I *truly* am, then I am better equipped to identify why I build walls and determine the best approach to break them down.

According to Emilie Griffin, in *Small Surrenders:*

> What must we do to clothe ourselves with a new self? In fact, this is a work of grace, which seemingly comes over us when we are attentive, faithful, and believing. This is the reason for our rejoicing: that Jesus came for us and gave us the way to imitate him, to imitate God. However inadequate we may feel to this amazing destiny, it is ours (who we are), it is the promise that Jesus has made to us and lived out for us. Our task is to accept the grace, to make our small surrenders.

My main purpose is to make God's name great, which in turn glorifies Him. When I am living this in my life, I am then fulfilling my purpose and living who I truly am.

Jericho Girls' Response: Can you identify with them?

- *I have been so wrapped up in my daily duties as a mother and wife; I can't identify who I truly am.*

- *Knowing who I am in Christ makes me feel satisfied and complete.*

- *Understanding Whose I am reveals to me my calling in life.*

Jericho Girls' Tool Box:

Quit *hammering* on yourself!

"Therefore, if anyone is in Christ, he is a new creation; the old has gone, the new has come!" (2 Corinthians 5:17).

Training Your Soul and Breaking Down Walls:

When you write things, they become more real. Write down the things that characterize you, as who you really are. What do you enjoy? What makes you tick? Once you have made a list, study it and begin to embrace and love who you really are because that is who God uniquely made you to be. Next, create a separate list of your attributes that are out of place in God's creation, and that should be purged. Once you have made this list, review it and begin to disassociate from these attributes that do not define who you really are. Finally, look through the book of Psalms. Which one speaks to you about who you are? Pick a Psalm denoting where you are with God in your walk today and pray it daily.

3

GETTING REAL
WITH GOD

GROWLY WITH GOD

Each morning I struggle with getting up early to get my alone time with God. As I write this book, I have made the commitment to get up even earlier so that I can have my alone time and then write. It is a struggle for me, to say the least, just to get up early. But to make the decision to wake up even earlier to write has been quite a feat. The alarm goes off at 5:00 a.m. and I grumble to God, "I hate this! It is so dark outside. It is cold and I don't want to get out of bed." Despite my complaints and growling at Him, my feet hit the floor. God knows my heart. He knows that I am not a morning person. Because He already knows, I can be very real with my emotions each morning. Once I get my coffee and get going, I love my time with Him and writing each day. However, I have the same experience each morning despite loving the end result.

My relationship with God has always been pretty darn real. I think it is mostly because I understand that He already knows my heart and its struggles, so talking with Him openly always seems to put things into perspective. However, there are still things that are difficult to be real about. One of them is to confront my failings before Him. One of my struggles is taming my tongue.

When I cannot speak my piece to someone or say what is on my mind, I wrestle with myself and it eats at me. I prefer to state what I am feeling to someone rather than hold back, but speaking my mind is not always the best approach. In fact, Scripture teaches us to be slow to speak. James 1:19 says; "My dear brothers (and sisters), take note of this; everyone should be quick to listen, slow to speak and slow to become angry." James 3 also talks about taming the tongue. So when I mess this up, I eventually confess this to God and return to being real with Him. I ask for wisdom and for the ability to speak well for Him. But bringing my failures before Him is the most difficult. It is easy to come to Him and pray for others and chat, but when it is time to be real and examine my heart, it is easier to skate around this and focus on other things. But that is what a relationship with Him should be, REAL. Bringing our faults, our dreams, our desires, disappointments, hurts, and failures all before Him. Giving everything to God, the good, the bad, and the ugly— that is how you begin to get *real* with God; and just maybe, it begins with a growl.

OUR GREATEST STRUGGLES

As I stand at the mountain top and yell "HELLO!" I hear an echo— "hello, hello, hello!" Is it just me or are there others out there who feel the same way? I asked the Jericho Girls what their biggest struggles were in getting real with God. The consensus: faith, trust, and control. Let's take a closer look.

Faith

To begin, let's first define what faith is. According to Merriam-Webster.com, faith is:

1. Firm belief in something for which there is no proof. Complete trust.

2. Belief and trust in and loyalty to God. Belief in the traditional doctrines of a religion.

Hebrews 11:1 states: "Now faith is confidence in what we hope for and assurance about what we do not see."

Presuming that God exists, once we believe in God, the next step is to understand the relation we should have with Him.

After just two years of marriage, my father-in-law suddenly died of a heart attack. He was only fifty-one years old when he died. The experience rocked my husband's world, his family's, and mine. Our family was shaken to the core. When someone is unexpectedly ripped out of your life with no chance for goodbyes or any type of closure, it is difficult. It left us stunned and asking "why". It tested our faith. Twenty years later, we still do not know *why* Dad was taken. The only thing we can hold tight to is that God must have had a very good reason that is beyond our comprehension. It requires faith—complete trust and confidence in someone or something. It requires faith in an unseen God. Faith that He is in control, and faith that he has our, and Dad's best interest, even when it doesn't appear that way.

John 11 tells the story of Jesus raising Lazarus from the dead. In John 11:11, Jesus tells His disciples that Lazarus has died but that they were going back to "wake him up." On the way, Lazarus' sister, Martha, meets Jesus on the road. Scripture tells us (v. 20) "When Martha heard that Jesus was coming, she went out to meet Him, but Mary stayed at home." But Mary . . . I wonder if Mary's faith was wavering at this point in time. Mary did not go to meet Jesus. Did she stay at home weeping and wondering, "Where were you, Jesus, when I needed you? Why, oh why, didn't you heal my brother? You have healed so many others, so why couldn't you have healed *my* sick brother?"

This Mary is the one who sat at the feet of Jesus and took in His every word. She adored Jesus. However in this moment, there was a BUT MARY point in her life. She was faced with a decision. Does she decide to walk in faith and believe in Jesus, or does she let her faith fade, forgetting all that she knows and has witnessed about Jesus? How could she greet the One who decided not to heal her sick brother?

After Martha met Jesus on the road, she went back home and told Mary that the Teacher had called for her. In a society where rabbis would not teach women, Jesus, the Teacher, had asked for Mary! It was a pivotal time in Mary's faith. "Do I go to Him, or do I stay here and let my faith dissipate?" BUT MARY . . . chose to go. Not only did she go, Scripture tells us she got up *quickly* and went to Him.

She finally meets Jesus on the road. The dramatic story unfolds when she reaches Him and falls at His feet weeping. "Lord, if you had been here, my brother would not have died." I can hear her heartbreak and I can feel her immense pain. I remember that same scenario in my life as I saw my father-in-law lying motionless on the gurney in the ER. As I stood at the foot of him I too wept. "Lord, if you had only been here, my father-in-law would not have died." I too had a BUT moment.

In my story, as in Mary's, we ultimately decided to follow Jesus despite the circumstances. That didn't mean that I liked the situation or understood it. The only thing I could grasp was, like Mary, what I *knew* about Jesus. In Mary's story, Jesus wept when He saw Mary's heartache. I suppose Jesus wept too when He felt mine, my husband's, and his family's heartache. We marched on in faith.

During that time, there were many raw emotions I shared with God—anger, sadness, emptiness and loss, confusion, and heartache. I was real with Him. I believe God honors our emotions. Like an abandoned child, He took me and loved me. Most of the time, I do not understand the unseen. I found this to be the place where faith and hope intersect. "For in this hope we were saved. But hope that is seen is no hope at all. Who hopes for what he already has? But if we hope for what we do not yet have, we wait for it patiently" (Romans 8:24–25).

Trust

To trust means:

Noun: a firm belief in the reliability, truth, ability, or strength of someone or something

Verb: believe in the reliability, truth, ability, or strength of

Where does trust come into play when we are being real with God? Trust happens when a relationship is built with someone. It happens over time. Trust is not something that is given to someone without some type of track record in your relationship with them. We believe that person to be trustworthy, reliable, and truthful.

When one builds their relationship with God, they begin to find that God is trustworthy. In his book, *The Good and Beautiful God,* James Bryan Smith states,

The God Jesus reveals would never do anything to harm us. He has no malice or evil intentions. He is completely good. And the fact that God is also all-knowing and all-powerful makes His goodness even better. I can trust God even if things look bleak. It does not matter that God is all-powerful or all-knowing if He is not all-good. If He isn't all-good, I will never be able to love and trust Him.

Jesus reveals to us a God who loves us and whom we can trust even if our circumstances don't look like it. When my husband was out of work, our circumstances looked bleak. We needed two incomes to cover our bills and our debt. I knew God would somehow provide, but how? I had to decide if I was going to trust the all-good God I had come to know and love. I was real with God. I told Him that I was scared and uncertain about our future. I had never made enough money to completely support the family. David was always the main provider. But now our circumstances were turned around. It was up to God to somehow provide me with the work needed to sustain us.

I had many moments of being real and expressing my doubts and lack of trust. But once I overcame that, I began to remember all the things God has done for us in the past. I had never truly been hungry nor had I ever slept on the streets and experienced true coldness. As I began to count my blessings, my blessings list got longer and longer. I began to see that God had been trustworthy in the past; now I had to decide if I would trust Him and believe He would continue to be trustworthy in my future.

God provided opportunities in my business for the next three years that brought us through this difficult time. We had to revamp our lifestyle and eliminate things, but my business grew in a declining real estate market and we made it through these difficult times.

It is alright to be real with God—to confess your doubts and lack of trust to Him. There comes a point in your faith walk where you need to decide if you truly trust Him and, in trust, move forward with Him. James Bryan Smith said,

> But as we come to know the good and beautiful God that Jesus knows, our struggles take on a whole new meaning. If God is truly good and is looking out for our good, then we can come to Him with complete honesty. We can practice honesty when we pray—baring our soul and confronting those hurts that make us doubt God's goodness by handing them over to him for healing.

"Trust in the LORD with all your heart and lean not on your own understanding; in all your ways acknowledge him, and he will make your paths straight" (Proverbs 3:5–6).

Being real with God means confessing our doubts, and then being able to move forward in trust. Because we are called to trust God with all our hearts, we need to bring down these walls. We cannot fully trust Him with untrusting walls in place.

Control

I consider myself to be a control freak. If I don't do it, it won't get done or won't get done right. I hear myself repeating this time and time again. If it is difficult for me to relinquish control to another, imagine how tough it is for me to give up control to God! So what do I do?

To begin, I needed to cut ties from the wrong thinking that I can do everything better. My way is not necessarily the best way all the time. (That was difficult to say.) This means that my thinking has to change when I attempt to control events in my life. I call myself a perfectionist, but it typically revolves around controlling my work. As a self-employed business woman in the real estate industry, I feel the need to control things in my business. What I have found is, when I truly examine myself, I have a similar struggle with releasing control to God. Some things I easily hand over to Him, knowing He is in control, while others I hold on tightly to.

When we cling to things or try to control circumstances in our lives, what we are saying is: "God, I can do this better than You. I've got this—no need for Your help today." I believe what God wants us to do is release everything into His sovereign control, knowing that we are truly not in control anyway.

As women, we attempt to control so many things. "If I can just watch my children a little bit closer, nothing will ever happen to them." "If I can control my husband a little bit better, nothing will ever go wrong in our marriage." "If I can hold on to my money a little bit tighter, I will always have enough." Ladies, we attempt to control everything!

For me, this meant acknowledging that I am not *truly* in control. And if I am not really in control, then what is the purpose of trying to control events that are out of my control anyway? Relinquishing control is one of the most difficult things to do, but it can become easier once we realize that God is the One who has ultimate control of our circumstances and our entire lives. Praying the prayer, "Not my will be done but Yours" is a difficult one. Especially when you are praying that for your loved one, your child, your husband, mom, dad, or . . .

Relinquishing these control issues to Him gives you the freedom to know that God is sovereign and in control and that you don't have to run the world. You can breathe a sigh of relief knowing that our all-good, all-loving God has "got this" and has our best interests at heart—even when we don't understand. Getting real with God about the things you attempt to control in your life looks like this:

1. Acknowledge before Him the things you attempt to control. You might want to make a list and work on the items one by one.

2. Talk with Him about your struggles of letting go. Tell Him you know that you are not capable of doing this alone, because you will relinquish control and then attempt to

take it back. He already knows your control issues. You are not alone. We all do it, release control to God and then take it back. It's a moment by moment struggle. Be honest and real about why you feel the need to control those things in your life.

3. Finally, continue to pray for the ability to give God total control of your life.

This, my friends, is a lifelong adventure!

WHO ELSE?

So who else struggled with these issues, yet became conquers?

Control: Abram (later renamed Abraham) is promised to be the father of many nations. (Genesis 15) Later, in Genesis 16, we see Sarai (later renamed Sarah) battling with control issues. Sarai doubts how her husband, Abram, will be the father of many nations if she cannot conceive a child. So she decides to take matters into her own hands. She tells Abram to sleep with her maidservant, Hagar (Genesis 16), who becomes pregnant and gives Abram a son. But this was not the son God promised Abram. Sarai ran ahead of God, taking control of the situation. As we find out later in Scripture, God had a better plan (of course). If only she had let God be in charge of her life, not running ahead, her future events would have been much easier. God's ways are always the best way.

Faith: Sarai lacked faith. She laughed when she heard that she would bear a child in her old age. (Genesis 18:1–15) When questioned why she laughed, she denied it. She chose not to be real with God. God blessed her anyway, with a son, just as He promised.

Trust: In Exodus 3, Moses argued with God three times. First, he said, "Who am I that I should go to Pharaoh and bring the Israelites out of Egypt?" Secondly, he asked, "Suppose I go to the Israelites and say to them, 'The God of your fathers has sent me to you,' and they ask me, 'What is his name?' Then what shall I tell them?" Lastly, "What if they do not believe me or listen to me and say, 'The Lord did not appear to you'?" Moses did not trust that God would do what

He had promised. Moses was real with God in bringing his concerns and fears before Him; but despite Moses' lack of trust, God blessed him anyway.

What do we learn from the lives of these people who struggled with whether or not to be real with God? We learn that God can bless us, even if we choose not to open up to Him, trust Him, or relinquish our false control to Him. God longs for relationship with us and blesses us even more so, when we share and reveal our true feelings to Him. We can be completely real with God. Remember that He is still holy and that we should come to Him respectfully.

We can be angry, but with reverence and honor. We can show true emotions because He knows them before we show them. Come before Him understanding who He truly is—One who loves us unconditionally, because His very nature is that of love. When we bring down our walls and begin to give Him our faith, trust, and control, then we are able to move forward in a closer relationship with Him without walls. As we do this, we will see that He is trust-worthy and we can place our hearts in His safe and loving hands. God treasures our hearts. Why not give yours over to Him?

JERICHO GIRLS' RESPONSE: CAN YOU IDENTIFY WITH THEM?

- *Getting real with God means that I have to tell Him I am scared or don't want to do something.*

- *Telling God I am angry is difficult for me.*

- *Getting real with God means trusting Him. If I do not trust Him, I am stating to Him that I can do things better than He can—and I know that is not true.*

Jericho Girls' Tool Box:

Let God *rule* your day.

"I will instruct you and teach you in the way you should go;
I will counsel you and watch over you" (Psalm 32:8).

Training Your Soul and Breaking Down Walls:

Trust God throughout your day. Relinquish control to Him each day. Have faith in what God can do. You might have to do these things hourly, or even minute by minute.

4

GETTING REAL WITH OTHERS

The Jericho Girls discussed getting real with others. The night we met for this discussion, fewer women showed up for the meeting. Why? Because it is a difficult topic to address. When we have to examine ourselves and search our hearts to determine why we can't be authentic, it is uncomfortable. We can discuss getting real with God, but discussing relationships among people in our daily living means getting real with each other and ourselves right then and there!

After the meeting, I received emails stating why each woman chose not to attend. They basically had the same answer: "I was afraid." Well, we are all afraid to deal with ourselves, but that is what this group is all about—examining our hearts and working to change them. In getting real with others, we studied three areas: experience, appearance, and shame. Our experiences in life either enable us or disable us from being real. How we appear to ourselves and to others weighs heavily on whether or not we are real. Shame inhibits us from reaching out and building true relationships.

EXPERIENCING WALLS OF HURT

When we began to explore our daily dealings with others, we started to realize that many of us do not fully share our hearts. We spend our lives peeking over our guarded walls to say "Hello." That is the extent of our connection with others. Why? Experience is one major factor. We carry our past and present experiences with us, both the good and the bad. When we pack those experiences into the beds of our trucks and drive them around with us, we allow the weight of these burdens to follow us everywhere we go. We have all been hurt by someone. In dealing with those hurts we have erected walls so tall, so thick, and so long that it is impossible to grasp what real connection looks like.

Can you remember a time when your heart was broken or a hurtful word was spoken? All of us can! Those experiences leave scars on our hearts. Our natural response is to place another brick on our wall to protect us so that no one will be able to hurt us again with further pain. Rejection by someone you love is a very difficult thing. A broken heart hurts, and hateful words linger. What do we do to protect ourselves from hurt? Chances are we will all eventually be hurt in a relationship, whether intentionally or not. Even the strongest marriages and friendships can involve hurt. It is what we do with those hurts that help us to move forward or get stuck. When we feel like we have been wronged, it is best to confront the situation and have dialogue with the other party. Maybe that person meant no harm, or maybe they did; but it is always best to make an effort to address the perceived hurt and attempt to reconcile. Understanding where the other person is coming from is vital. Only then can we make our best decision in a relationship and move forward.

Many of us live our lives behind our walls and say, "I am done." While this reaction is one that many choose, it leaves us bitter and alone.

God did not create us to be without relationships. We are created in His image; He wants us in relationship with Him and in community. After man was created, the Lord God said, "It is not good that the man should be alone; I will make him a helper fit for him" (Genesis 2:18). God tells us it is not good for us to be alone. Therefore this is not a godly option. If you are confined behind a wall of hurt because of past or present experiences, it is time to make a change. Begin to pray about your hurts—talk to our Father about them. When you feel alone, know that you are not. God is with you. He is for you. Deuteronomy 31:6 says, "Be strong and courageous. Do not be afraid or terrified because of them, for the LORD your God goes with you; He will never leave you nor forsake you."

LIVING WITH PRIDE

We all have someone in our lives who will help us and who loves us, but we have to ask for help. I asked a few of my friends why we do not ask for help. They all had the same answer—pride. We don't want our friends to know anything is wrong, and we certainly don't want them to think that we need help. That would make us *appear* weak. They also said they don't want to be the "needy" friend. We probably have all had the needy friend or have been the needy friend who can be a life sucker. This type of person drains. Having a few close friends is important so that we don't wear one another out.

As I talk about asking for help, I am saying that when needed, reach out to someone you know and trust, and admit that you need help. We should draw on our friends' strengths when we feel weak. We can also draw from God, who is the ultimate source of our strength.

I discussed pride with friends that I have known for years. They all had the same response: pride robs us of asking for help. How could friends be so close, yet so far away? What is wrong with weakness? God delights in weakness, because it is through weakness He can make us strong. In weakness He can grow us and stretch us. If we allow ourselves to run to Him through tough times, He will give us peace beyond all understanding. It is through that peace that others will see that even in tough circumstances, there is something different about us. We react differently than others do when we are pressed or even crushed by life's circumstances. We have the peace of Jesus. When we have that, the world looks dim as we shine. "But He said to me, 'My grace is sufficient for you, for my power is made perfect in weakness.' Therefore I will boast all the more gladly about my weaknesses, so that Christ's power may rest on me. That is why, for Christ's sake, I delight in weaknesses, in insults, in hardships, in persecutions, in difficulties. For when I am weak, then I am strong" (2 Corinthians 12:9–10).

Do you delight in weakness? I don't! It is difficult. But we should, because when we do, we are made strong. Andy Stanley said, "God may show His power on the stage of your weakness." I love this, because I often think that God has to show power through my strength in life. But instead, He chooses to reveal His Power and Glory through frailty. In order to be real with others, we need to let down our guards, open up to our friends and ask for help. We need to work on our fear of being weak and begin to dismantle our walls—brick by brick, stone by stone. There is no time limit on how long a wall should take to come down. Only God knows that. Ultimately, we know that we cannot live behind walls and be real with God or others. Being stuck behind a wall is a tough place to be and it may seem impossible to get out from behind it. But we need to start, because until we do, we will be missing out on the life that has been intended for us by the One who created us.

When David and I went through our financially difficult time, it was hard to ask for help. We had always been the ones who helped others—not the other way around. I was forced into a new way of thinking. The truth was, I needed help. I went to my closest friends and asked for emotional help. On one visit with them, I began to discuss our situation and started crying. I was tired of trudging forward alone in this financial mess. I was scared. They both sat there, unable to say anything. They were used to me listening to them and being the strong one. But now, there I was before them, a sobbing mess. My one friend said to me, "You can't break down like this, you are Elmer—our Elmer's glue. You keep *us* together." We all broke out in laughter. My past experience taught me that I was a giver. I was the strong one. Everyone could come to me and I would be there, ready to help. But what I learned from our financial struggle is that my friends were there for me, ready to take me in, listen to me, and watch me completely fall apart. Getting real with them helped me grow, bring down my wall, and show them my heart, which was in need of love and care. It assured me that they were there for me. It grew me in a way that spoke to my heart. "You, Dawna dear, cannot do life on your own!" We need to harness our good and bad experiences in life. Use the good and filter out the bad. Get correct narratives and know that it is good to share with someone who is trustworthy. Get real with them.

Recently, I was talking with a friend who discovered that she had a tumor. She quickly became sick, and, after surgery, developed an infection. Like me, my friend is a self-employed business woman; and when she is "down", her business is too. I asked her, "What did you do?" She responded, "I had to get rid of my pride. I could not get myself to ask for help, but fortunately I have family and friends who just stepped in." She needed monetary assistance with hospital bills not covered by insurance. She needed help with her child and running her household. She needed help maintaining her business. She told me that it was even more difficult accepting the gracious gifts of love. Even though she did not ask for help, her loved ones stepped up and assisted her. She said, "My pride kept me hostage from asking for help. I had to swallow my pride and accept the help that was graciously given to me. It was even difficult for me to simply say thank you."

Being real with others begins with acknowledging hurts, recognizing that we have an extremely difficult time asking for help, and admitting to ourselves that we can be prideful. When we are transparent with others, they see the real us. What I have found is that they generally like what they see. It shows that we all have similar struggles and need each other. What better way to walk through life than transparently together?

APPEARANCE

Throughout the ages, beauty has always reigned. We live in a society of comparison that tells us we are never enough. Media ads bombard us daily with lies telling us that being beautiful, skinny, wrinkle free, and appearing youthful affirms our worth. Having more things will make us happy. Magazine ads inundate us with gorgeous girls, air brushed to perfection. I saw a billboard with a beautiful woman on a Harley motorcycle which implied, *get the bike, you will get this girl!* But the truth of the matter is that our outward appearance or the possessions we have do not give us our worth. Who we are on the inside and belonging to Christ gives us our worth. Proverbs 31 tells us:

A wife (or Woman) of noble character who can find?
She is worth far more than rubies.
Her husband has full confidence in her
and lacks nothing of value.
She brings him good, not harm,
all the days of her life.
She selects wool and flax
and works with eager hands.
She is like the merchant ships,
bringing her food from afar.
She gets up while it is still dark;
she provides food for her family
and portions for her female servants.
She considers a field and buys it;
out of her earnings she plants a vineyard.
She sets about her work vigorously;
her arms are strong for her tasks.
She sees that her trading is profitable,
and her lamp does not go out at night.
In her hand she holds the distaff
and grasps the spindle with her fingers.
She opens her arms to the poor
and extends her hands to the needy.
When it snows, she has no fear for her household;
for all of them are clothed in scarlet.
She makes coverings for her bed;
she is clothed in fine linen and purple.
Her husband is respected at the city gate,
where he takes his seat among the elders of the land.
She makes linen garments and sells them,
and supplies the merchants with sashes.
She is clothed with strength and dignity;
she can laugh at the days to come.
She speaks with wisdom,
and faithful instruction is on her tongue.
She watches over the affairs of her household
and does not eat the bread of idleness.

Her children arise and call her blessed;
her husband also, and he praises her:
"Many women do noble things,
but you surpass them all."
Charm is deceptive, and beauty is fleeting;
but a woman who fears the LORD is to be praised.
Honor her for all that her hands have done,
and let her works bring her praise at the city gate.

This passage tells us what gives us worth and beauty. A noble woman is hard to find. Why? First, we need to define the word "noble." Meriam-Webster.com defines the word this way: *possessing outstanding qualities *very good or excellent *grand or impressive especially in appearance *possessing, characterized by, or arising from superiority of mind or character or of ideals or morals.

What mental image do you picture when you think of this woman? I see a woman with great self-confidence, head held high, but not prideful. I see her as eloquently dressed, tasteful, beautiful inside and out, a woman who speaks with love and grace and who is wise. One who loves herself, is a leader, and builds up all who are around her. I want to be this woman of noble character—don't you?

She is magnificent, and that is only the first line of the whole scripture! Let's look at the rest of the scripture.

- Her intent is always good, not destructive.

- She is a hard worker.

- She is a business woman.

- She embraces the poor and needy—she makes time for others.

- She has no fear when storms come because she is grounded in God.

- Her husband is respected by others (I believe because she has built this man up and respected him in the highest way possible, her husband in turn feels respect and has a high self-esteem. The husband exudes this and others respect him at the city gates.)

- She laughs—she is filled with joy.

- She is strong but is not afraid to share her weaknesses.

- She controls her tongue.

- She spends time on eternal affairs—things that matter for eternity.

- Her husband and children love, respect, and praise her.

- She fears God.

- She will be stunning her whole life, even when her physical beauty fades.

- She is honored.

I also see her as one who does not focus on her outward appearance or worry what others think or say. Do you see how this starkly contrasts the way the world sees beauty?

Why is this woman so hard to find? First, the world teaches us the opposite—our outer beauty is what matters. However, this scripture paints a whole different picture of what makes this woman different. I believe that, first and foremost, she fears God in a Holy way. She is accountable to Him, and only Him. When she is accountable to God, her whole viewpoint about who she is shifts. She sees things through God's eyes. She has the fear of God. Once God is in focus, everything else she does and says comes from the perspective of God.

How can we model our lives in such a grandiose way that we become like this woman of noble character? We need to quit worrying about our physical appearance. We need to quit worrying about what others think about us. We feel beautiful because we are. We are each created in God's image. We are fearfully and wonderfully made (Psalm 139:14). God made us all unique beings, in His own image. You are perfectly beautiful just the way you are. You and I can apply the principles of Proverbs 31 to live our lives in such a dynamic way that we will be this stunning woman of noble character. We need to start seeing ourselves as God sees us.

Another form that appearance takes on is "false appearance", appearing to be perfect in front of others. In doing this, it builds walls rather than bridges.

I was at a woman's luncheon where two older women introduced themselves and began to have a conversation. They seemed to hit it off right from the start. Julia began to discuss her wonderful daughter-in-law to Nancy. She shared the loving relationship she had with her daughter-in-law and stated she was so blessed. Nancy then shared that she did not have a close relationship with her daughter-in-law and wished that she had the closeness that Julia had. I glanced from a distance, watching the two converse for some time, but it seemed as if they never *truly* connected.

After the conversation ended, I spoke to Julia. She shared with me how she enjoyed speaking to Nancy. She told me how they discussed their relationships with their daughters-in-law. Julia looked at me and said, "Of course I didn't tell her about my *other* daughter-in-law and my lack of relationship with her." I thought, *Why not?* Julia had an incredible opportunity to connect with Nancy and share her same struggles. Even though she has a wonderful relationship with one daughter-in-law, she struggles to connect with the other. Maybe Nancy needed encouragement that day. Nancy was transparent and Julia was not.

Julia chose to hide behind a wall of false appearance, attempting to look perfect. She was not transparent for fear of how she might appear to someone else. She was so concerned with how she appeared to Nancy that she missed an incredible opportunity to see what the Father was up to. She missed an opportunity to be real with another woman of God, an opportunity to connect in a powerful way. Ultimately, she missed out on God's gift of encouragement.

It is easy to judge Julia, but we all do this. We miss out. We miss out because we are worried about how we look to others. Let's commit to being real with one another.

Ladies, we need to pause here and ponder this important point. Without sharing and being transparent, we build walls of false appearance. Julia did not have to share every detail with this woman. After all, she just met her. But, she could have let God use a part of her story so that Nancy could get a glimpse of her, and potentially, Jesus! When people see Jesus in you, they are attracted to you.

I had a woman email me and say she was afraid to be real and open up because if she did, others would not like her. The truth of the matter is, we all have things that we are not proud of or too ashamed to let others see. BUT JESUS cleansed us from all unrighteousness, and we have been washed clean. We should show others the "BUT Jesus" side of us. In doing so, it allows us to be real with each other and make true connections. When we say, "Yeah, my life was or is a mess BUT JESUS is doing a new work in me," we begin to see that it is not by our efforts but by God's grace and mercy that He has made our appearance beautiful. Christ's blood cleanses all.

So ladies, let's not hide behind walls of false appearance. Let's be real and say, "I am not perfect, BUT Christ is! He died for me and is working in me in a mighty way. I am a work in progress. If someone doesn't like me or where I am in my walk, then they are probably not a true friend."

Being real will open the door to powerful friendships and to meaningful, lasting relationships. The kind that God has intended for our lives. So, be real and say "NO" to pretending.

SHAME

Get rid of shame. When my friend, Tamera, led our Jericho Girls session on "Getting Real with Others", she brought to light the fact that we all carry around shame. I love how God used her experiences to teach us about the burdens of carrying around shame. She said that shame keeps us frozen behind our walls and does not allow a true connection with others.

There are many causes of shame, including past and present experiences—things we have done wrong or turned out wrong in spite of good intentions. But God can miraculously heal those experiences, so that we no longer live in shame but in light of what He has done in our lives. We are special because God made us all unique. The sum of our experiences, good and bad, define us as the incredible creatures we are.

On the flip side, we can sometimes see ourselves as performing better than we are. Sometimes we are so caught up in performance that we fail to see we are not living out what we preach. This is when we truly need a trusted spiritual mentor to talk with. Self-examination is a good spiritual discipline that should be exercised every so often, to see where we are improving and failing in our walk with God.

As we journey to Jericho, we are encouraged to spend time in prayer with the Father and ask Him, "Where am I excelling in my faith walk, and where am I failing?" Most recently, God has been revealing to me that I am failing in sharing love—particularly with a few specific people in my life. Everything I read recently has been on loving others well. So I spend time in prayer, and work on loving well. First with God, then others—even when I don't *feel* like it. God is showing me (since I am definitely a work in progress) that when I don't love well, I build walls. Then I begin to feel shameful. Shameful before God because, as a maturing Christian, I am still failing in such an important area such as LOVE!

So, whether we feel shame for past mistakes and hide from others, or feel shameful before God, both situations call for moving from behind that wall, forgiving ourselves, and loving well so that we can live complete lives. Confessing and working on this during alone time with Him is essential.

We also need to share our fears and disappointments with our close friends. We believe that if we dare to share our setbacks and disappointments, even the shameful ones, we would not be lovable. Shame destroys. The enemy uses this to his advantage. When we feel shame for something in our lives, we simply turn it into a secret. Marilyn Meberg said,

> The reason it is so hard for us to admit to the secrets hidden in our hearts is that we're ashamed of them. We think that if we keep denying our ugly stuff then maybe we'll look better than we fear we actually are. We keep it a secret. And those secrets can fester and swell until they consume our happiness and our hope. From her blog, Devotionals Daily, The Shame Monster.

Secrets keep us prisoner in a jail of loneliness. When you are able to share, know that you are not alone. There are many women who have had similar experiences in life that cause them to hide and keep secrets. Eventually, they build a wall of shame around their hearts.

Some experiences need the wise counsel of a therapist who can help them deal with deep issues. In those cases, we need to seek professional faith believing therapists.

From childhood experiences to our actions as adults, each event and experience can create shame in our lives that shapes who we are and adds more layers to the walls we build. Housing shame in our hearts is not God's desire for us! Do you remember the movie, *The Help?* Mini gives a *special pie* to Hilly which appears to be a peace offering—but it is not. It is something very different. After many years of hiding the thing she did to Hilly, Mini finally decides that she needs to share the "terrible awful thing" she did to Mrs. Hilly with her friends. She could no longer hide the shameful secret. Mini found healing in sharing with her trusted friends.

How do we heal from this shameful perception we have of ourselves?

- Open our hearts to God's love.
- Share what is hidden deep inside our hearts to someone we trust.
- Acknowledge our own false narratives.
- Take on God's character of Love and learn to love and forgive ourselves.

How do we begin to get real with others and slowly dismantle our walls? Again, search your heart to see where you need improvement. List how you need to be real, in what areas, and then begin the process. Get real with yourself first, then you will have more freedom to get real with others.

WHOSE OPINION SHALL PREVAIL?

We need to spend less time worrying about what others think and more time caring about what God thinks. A mature sister shared her experience with me, of how she attempted to be perfect with one of her adult children. When she would visit him, she stated, "I was always trying to be *God's perfect* representative for my son and his wife. I thought that if I could be perfect in front of them, they would see me as the *model Christian mother* and they would think I was wonderful." As our discussion continued, we discussed worrying more about what God thinks rather than what others think. If we get our perspective correct—truly living for God and only caring about His opinion, rather than others—we will enable our spirit to maintain a right alignment with His. When my mature sister decided to live for God, rather than attempting to be *perfect* for her children, she realized that she *was* a better role model because she had the correct motives.

Living for God's approval based on performance is NOT what works. Checking for His approval, by examining your heart before Him, being in communion with Him, and being at His feet will truly make you the woman that God wants you to be. Opening up to trustworthy friends and being real helps to connect us and aids in sharing our true selves with others.

Whose opinion is most important to you? Whose opinion will prevail in your heart? How would the way you live be different if you didn't depend on how you appeared to others, and were only concerned with what God thought?

JERICHO GIRLS' RESPONSE: CAN YOU IDENTIFY WITH THEM?

- *I chose not to attend this particular meeting because getting real with others is one of the scariest things for me to do. If others see who I really am, they will not like what they see. So I decided to sit this one out.*

- *I definitely have walls of shame. I feel inadequate to fully discuss and give answers during group discussions because I believe I am not smart enough or have the right answers. How can I be real with others if I can't be real enough to discuss and share in a group?*

JERICHO GIRLS' TOOL BOX:

Quit **wrenching** on yourself!

"I am fearfully and wonderfully made; your works are wonderful" (Psalm 139:14).

TRAINING YOUR SOUL AND BREAKING DOWN WALLS:

See yourself as God sees you—one who is worthy of His Love. Each time you are hard on yourself, remember that God delights in you! Spend some time in Psalm 139. Remind yourself that you are "fearfully and wonderfully made."

5

WALLS OF HURT

HURT IS A REAL FEELING

Hurt is a vast topic, ranging from minor hurts, to hurts that run so deep, that it seems impossible to scratch the surface. Veins of hurt can grow from the deepest part of our hearts. Some begin during our childhood. Sometimes we don't even know they exist. Being hurt and feeling the effects of it is a real physical feeling. In an article from *Scientific American,* Robert Emery and Jim Coan discuss the feeling of "heartache" and "gut-wrenching" as both physical and emotional pain. They state that both physical and emotional pain involve the same brain regions. Even though scientists do not know the exact pathways involved, they have discovered that there is a correlation and that the two seem to be intimately connected. Emery and Coan also state that heartache is not the only way emotional and physical pain interacts in our brain:

Recent studies show that even experiencing emotional pain on behalf of another person—that is, empathy—can influence our pain perception. And this empathy effect is not restricted to humans. In 2006 a paper published in Science revealed that when a mouse observes its cage mate in agony, its sensitivity to physical pain increases. And when it comes into close contact with a friendly, unharmed mouse, its sensitivity to pain diminishes.

Soon after, one of us (Coan) published a functional MRI study in humans that supported the finding in mice, showing that simple acts of social kindness, such as holding hands, can blunt the brain's response to threats of physical pain and thus lessen the experience of pain.

This article was the inspiration for the "training of our soul" activity, which is performing simple acts of kindness. This training included reaching out to someone—saying or doing something kind for another person. We set goals: "This week I will reach out to one person and the next I will reach out to three." This comprised simple gestures; holding someone's hand or sharing a hug. So we began "training our souls and breaking down walls" by doing simple acts of kindness for others, thus testing the idea that simple acts of kindness help in the healing process for the hurts of life's wounds. Not too long after our session on *Walls of Hurt*, the news reported a huge tragedy: A gunman entered Sandy Hook Elementary School in Newtown, Connecticut, and killed twenty children and six adults. The world was left shaken! What happen next surprised me—reports of people doing acts of kindness to heal the hurt of the tragedy our nation was dealing with.

What we have found is that we can begin to heal our own wounds and hurts by simply helping others. Acts of kindness help us to focus our attention on others and not wallow in our own hurts, thus aiding in bringing down our walls.

DROPPED

We began to study the story of David, the shepherd boy becoming king, and his experiences with hurt. After the death of King Saul and his son Jonathan (David's best friend), Abner was murdered by Joab (2 Samuel 3:22–38). Abner was the cousin of Saul and the commander-in-chief of Saul's army. Word spread of Abner's death and "all of Israel became alarmed" (2 Samuel 4:1). Because there was no other claimant to the throne from the house of Saul and with the news that Abner had died, the people were frightened and began to flee.

Now Jonathan, son of Saul had a son who was five years old when the news came about King Saul and Jonathan. "His nurse picked him up and fled, but as she hurried to leave, he fell and became crippled. His name was Mephibosheth" (2 Samuel 4:4). Mephibosheth was crippled in both feet after this incident. To be crippled is an extremely difficult thing. We can be crippled physically and we can be crippled emotionally. Being crippled emotionally typically involves being "dropped" or hurt by someone we love and trust, and leaves us dealing with a lifetime of scars.

Mephibosheth was dropped physically. As a result, he probably lived his childhood being ridiculed and treated different because of his disability. This, in turn, might have led to Mephibosheth feeling like he was crippled emotionally and socially as well. We too can identify with Mephibosheth. All of us, at one time or another, have been dropped. Can you identify a time in your life when you've been dropped? Has it crippled you emotionally? When we are dropped, we construct walls around our hearts to defend against being hurt again. Next we begin to isolate ourselves. The truth is, we are always at risk of being hurt. The only one who does not hurt us is God. People may fail us, but God never will. We need to decide if we are willing to allow others in despite the risk of hurt, or build, yet another wall of isolation.

ACTS OF KINDNESS

As the story unfolds, David becomes king of Israel. As God blesses King David's rule over Israel, David remembers his promise to his best friend Jonathan (I Samuel 20). So, he asks if he can show kindness to his best friend's family. David is told that Jonathan's son, Mephibosheth is alive but is lame in both feet. David wants to take him in and care for him. At this point, I wonder if I were in David's situation, if I would have said, "send for him" or if I would've thought:

Wow, I want to show kindness and keep my promise, but this seems like an overwhelming responsibility—to care for my friend's crippled

53

son. But not David; he sent for Mephibosheth. When Mephibosheth comes into the presence of King David, David tells him not to be afraid and restores Mephibosheth's inheritance to him. He performs an act of kindness, and not just a one time event. David takes Mephibosheth into his home and cares for him for the rest of his life. I suppose this act of kindness helped heal and restore his broken heart over the loss of Jonathan and King Saul.

BETRAYAL AND HURT

We now jump forward in the story. Much has transpired in David's life from the time David takes in Mephibosheth to what we will read next. There has been turmoil within David's family: Amnon and Tamar; David's affair with Bathsheba; David's son Absalom, has killed his brother Amnon—(2 Samuel 10-15). Now we peek forward to a time in David's life where his third son, Absalom, attempts to take over the kingdom.

Absalom had convinced the people that he should be king. David gets word of this and flees Jerusalem with his officials. While on the run, Ziba, the steward of Mephibosheth, approaches David and informs him that Mephibosheth is staying in Jerusalem in hopes that, "The house of Israel will give me back my grandfather's kingdom". At this point, David grants Ziba all of Mephibosheth's inheritance (2 Samuel 16: 1–4).

Do you suppose David felt betrayed by Mephibosheth? Do you suppose he wondered why Mephibosheth would hurt and betray him like this after he had taken him in, cared for him, and given him his inheritance? As the story unfolds, Absalom is killed and David finds himself returning to Jerusalem to reclaim his kingdom.

As David returns to the palace, Mephibosheth meets David on the road. We pick up the story in 2 Samuel 19:24–30. Scripture tells us that Mephibosheth had not washed his clothes, trimmed his mustache or taken care of his feet from the day the king left until he returned home safely. When they meet on the road, David asks Mephibosheth, "Why didn't you go with me"? Mephibosheth responds that he wanted to, but because he is lame in his feet, he needed to saddle up a donkey but Ziba betrayed him and would not let him go.

David then orders Mephibosheth's inheritance to be split between him and his servant, Ziba, but Mephibosheth says that Ziba can have it all. As long as his king is home safely, he is good.

It is difficult to decipher who is telling the truth; but from reading Mephibosheth's account and response to King David, it seems that Mephibosheth was telling the truth. He did not take advantage of King David's offer and seemed to be truly happy that the king returned to the palace. Do you suppose David felt like he could not trust either of them? I wonder if David felt betrayed by both persons he showed kindness to. Would they hurt him again? Regardless, he continued to love Mephibosheth and care for him. He kept his promise. David made a decision to move forward despite the hurt.

We can get stuck there—in the hurt—if we allow ourselves to stay there. We need to decide if we want to continue the relationship or not. We need to decide how much of our heart we are risking, and then evaluate the cost of that risk. Once we decide what to do, we can move forward. Love is risky, but when we set boundaries with others and then carefully move forward, either with or without that person in our lives, then we can live within protective healthy walls. Not walls of hurt or isolation. David chose to move forward with Mephibosheth.

A quote from the movie, *The Vow*, "Life's all about moments of *impact* and how they change our lives forever." This was a moment of impact for David. Being hurt by both Ziba and Mephibosheth (regardless of who was telling the truth), was a moment of impact—a moment in time when David could have gotten mad, remove both of them from his life, and decide not to deal with this. He could have chosen to be hurt and built walls around his heart. Instead, he decided to love, to forgive, and to continue his relationship with Mephibosheth.

OUR RESPONSE

How should we respond when we are hurt? What did Jesus say to do?

- Love your enemies—Mathew 5:43–45: "You have heard that it was said, 'Love your neighbor and hate your enemy'. But I tell you: Love your enemies and pray for those who persecute you, that you may be sons of your Father in heaven. He causes His sun to rise on the evil and the good, and sends rain on the righteous and the unrighteous."

- Do good to those who hate you. Luke 6:27

- Bless those who curse you. Luke 6:28

- Pray for those who mistreat you. Luke 6:28

- Do to others as you would have them do to you. Luke 6:31

Why should we do this? It sounds backwards, doesn't it? But this is how healing begins—by forgiveness and love. Forgiveness is for us—not the offending party. Love is shown to *all*, just as God loves us all. We do this because God tells us to and it works! We change, and with our hearts more like Jesus, God is pleased. We begin to love in a way we have never known; like God loves. Forgiving and loving someone doesn't mean you have to have them in your life. Through prayer, you decide whether or not to continue the relationship. Either way, you are choosing what is best for you.

This means you can forgive and decide for yourself if you want to have a relationship with that person or not. It gives you the power to decide who has access to your heart and who does not. If you do not continue the relationship, you can continue to pray for that person. You can choose kind words and show love in a mighty way no matter what. This helps build walls of love and keeps walls of hurt demolished.

You can also decide to have someone in your life, loving and forgiving them without hanging out with them. For example, if I have a family member whom I love, but I don't like their actions, I don't have to be best friends with that person. Because they are in my family, I simply cannot remove them from my life. Nevertheless, I don't have to hang out with them either. My pastor, Phil Vaughan gave an amazing sermon, "Not Your Average Joe," on the life of Joseph. He said, and I am paraphrasing, "Joseph chose to forgive his brothers from selling him into slavery. But after he forgave them, we never read in Scripture that he went on any camping trips in the desert with his brothers." Joseph loved his brothers, but the truth was that Joseph knew he could not trust them. If they were capable of selling him into slavery, would they hurt him again? Maybe and maybe not. But I presume that Joseph decided to play it smart and just see them at family functions.

My friend, Lauren Miller, writes in her book, *Hearing His Whisper,* "Love is the only thing you get to bring with you. . . in the end, nothing else matters. If you have love, you have everything."

She also states, "There are two kinds of people in life; those who are overcome and those *who overcome.* We do not have control as to what comes our way in life, but we can choose how we respond to it."

I love these two statements. Nothing else is more important in life than the ability to love as God does. You will be able to get past people who have hurt you, because people who hurt have typically been hurt. To love like Jesus is the only way. The overcomer or the overcome; which one are you? Whom will you choose to be today? Overcome your walls of hurt. It is the only way to live freely.

Joseph chose to love his brothers after being sold into Egyptian slavery. Years later, when confronting his brothers, he says in Genesis 45:4–5, "Come close to me." When they had done so, he said, "I am your brother Joseph, the one you sold into Egypt! And now, do not be distressed and do not be angry with yourselves for selling me here, because it was to save lives that God sent me ahead of you." Joseph forgave his brothers, disassembled his walls of hurt, and loved them. But he also made wise choices about where he would and would not hang out with them. Joseph chose to view his misfortune from God's perspective. The choice is always ours. Will you choose to love after being hurt?

Reflect on the wedding vows that Paige and Leo made to each other in the movie, *The Vow:*

> *Paige:* "I vow to help you love life, to always hold you with tenderness and to have the patience that love demands, to speak when words are needed and to share the silence when they are not, and to live within the warmth of your heart and always call it home."

Leo: "I vow to fiercely love you in all your forms, now and forever. I promise to never forget that this is a once in a lifetime love."

God's love is a once in a lifetime love. Make a vow to Him today to love like He does. Forgive like He does. Bring down your wall of hurt and choose wisely.

Have you asked Jesus to come into your life? Do you know what this "vow" means?

The problem is sin. We have all made poor choices, mistakes, and simply messed up in life. The Bible tells us, "For all have sinned and fall short of the Glory of God" (Romans 3:23). Sin, disobedience to God separates us from Him. But the Bible also tells us, that God loves us so much, that He sent His son Jesus Christ to die for our sin. He was raised from the dead, and through faith when we accept His free gift of salvation, we become "well" spiritually and live forever with Him.

If you have never invited Jesus to come into your life, all you have to do is repeat a prayer like this one:

Jesus,

I do believe You are the Son of God, that You died on the cross, and rose from dead, to pay the penalty for my sin.

I invite You to come into my life, forgive my sin, and make me a part of the family of God. Come into my life and take control of it.

Thank you for Your gift of eternal life and for Your Holy Spirit, Who has come to live in me.

I ask this in Jesus' name.

Amen!

If you have said this prayer for the very first time, know that the God of the universe heard your prayer, has forgiven you, and you will live with Him throughout eternity.

As we acknowledge that hurt is a real feeling, know that you will never be "dropped" by God. Do acts of kindness to aid in healing. Forgive and love as God does, then you will begin to live without walls of hurt.

Jericho Girls' Response: Can you identify with them?

- *It is difficult to love after being hurt. Where does one begin?*

- *I do not have many friends anymore because it is hard for me to trust.*

- *Prayer is the beginning of healing.*

Jericho Girls' Tool Box:

Sister, *level* with yourself. Are hurts truly as bad as you think they are? If they are, can you decide to face them, forgive them, and move on?

"Weeping may endure for a night but joy comes in the morning" (Psalm 30:5).

Training Your Soul and Breaking Down Walls:

Do a simple act of kindness for someone. Reach out to someone, say or do something kind. This can be a simple gesture; holding someone's hand or sharing a hug. Forgive someone who has deeply hurt you. Begin to pray for that person.

6

WALLS OF ESTEEM

Esteem is another ginormous wall that takes work and effort to break down. Our self-esteem begins to develop early in our childhood. It is there where it began to grow and it is deeply rooted in our hearts and minds. It can take a lifetime to change wrong thinking about ourselves. The following principles are ones we need to incorporate into our daily thinking so that we can live and be the women God created us to be.

- We need to embrace our conceived imperfections. Conceived imperfections physically—the shape of my nose. Conceived imperfections of my personality, for me, my serious nature. Embracing all the things we dislike about ourselves, both externally and internally, gives us a healthy self-esteem and radiates our true beauty.

- We need to quit worrying about what others think.

- We need to practice worship before God that is pure.
- Begin correct self-talk.

BEAUTY BELOW THE SURFACE

When we study pieces of marble and granite, we see the beauty in the veining and detailing of the stone. When we purchase marble or granite, we find that the most expensive pieces are those with large veining, called "movement", which creates character in the stone. When we analyze what creates that beauty in the stone, we see that it is actually arises from impurities, heat, and time. These are the things in our lives that we typically do not like: *impurities*—bad choices and mistakes; *heat*—tests and trials; *time*—patience and waiting on God. These elements create in us the beautiful veining that makes us so precious and priceless.

How can impurities be beautiful? That is what God sees when He looks at you and me. God views us as beautiful. He only sees the veining within us and not the thing that caused the veining.

Recently I picked up some stones while hiking, and I journalled while observing one particular stone. Here is what I wrote, "I see sparkling pieces within hidden crevices of a dull, jagged, ragged rock. It has lines of orange and brown color that add beauty to the stone. There are irregular shapes of the rock from where it has been broken. The brokenness makes it unique and beautiful."

As we journey to Jericho and dismantle our unhealthy walls of Esteem, we need to remind ourselves that we are beautiful. In fact, God thinks our irregularities and our brokenness is beautiful. Because God sees us in this way, we need to begin to love and see ourselves in the same light.

How do we define esteem? Merriam-Webster.com defines it as, "The regard in which one is held; worth and value." Do you regard yourself with worth and value? Do you respect and admire yourself? We can have a healthy self-image or an unhealthy self-image. There is a difference between the two.

An unhealthy self-image says, "I am not beautiful, I have no worth, I don't believe in myself, God would not use someone like me." An unhealthy self-image can also take on the form of pride and might say, "Look what I have accomplished on my own, I can do all things myself, I deserve this—spend it all on yourself." It says, "I don't want anyone to see the real me *or*, I don't have walls." Unhealthy self-image is destructive and creates walls of unhealthy self-esteem. True!

Healthy self-image says, "Yes, I mess things up daily, but Christ is changing me." It says, "I am fearfully and wonderfully made; I am a new creation in Christ." It says, "I will be real and not worry about what others think. I love how God created me, I know who I am and whose I am."

It is time to begin to embrace your conceived imperfections and simply love yourself. You are a gorgeous, high quality, precious stone made from the trials of life and hand crafted by God. We need to embrace and utilize our imperfections.

We begin to do this by accepting and loving who we are—both externally and internally. As we embrace all that we are comprised of, we begin to see ourselves as the precious marble that has beautiful veining and love what we see. Loving the beauty below the surface is the way we build healthy walls of self-esteem.

DANCE WITHOUT A CARE ABOUT WHAT OTHERS THINK

This statement comes up time and time again—"Quit worrying what others think!" When the Jericho Girls discussed this topic, one of our *girls* said, "I recognize that I constantly compare myself to others and worry about what others think." In response, another said, "I don't see that in you—do you know why? Because I am sitting here thinking she is so good with others—and while you are talking, I am comparing myself to *you*." The group got a big laugh out of this. But isn't it true? We spend too much of our time comparing ourselves to others and being afraid of what others think of us. What does God's word say about our esteem and not worrying about what others think? Let's look at the story of King David as he brings the Ark of the Covenant to Jerusalem. But before we look at Scripture, let's sum up King David's life to this point.

David was a shepherd who was anointed by the prophet Samuel when he was a young boy (1 Samuel 16:1–13). He is then called into

63

King Saul's service, but Saul becomes jealous of David (1 Samuel 18). Saul is so jealous that he becomes obsessed with killing David (1 Samuel 19). David, fearing for his life, flees from Saul and is on the run for many years (1 Samuel 21–30). Saul eventually takes his own life (1 Samuel 31). In the course of time, David is anointed King over Hebron, Judah, and reigns there for seven years (2 Samuel 2). In 2 Samuel 5, we see King David now being anointed over Israel. Eventually he conquers Jerusalem, where he reigned for 33 years. During the reign of Saul, the ark had remained in Kiriath Jearim. In 2 Samuel 6, we see that David has decided to bring the ark back to Jerusalem. This is where we pick up the story.

He decides to transport the ark on a cart, which is in direct contradiction to the instructions for carrying the ark that God gave in Exodus 25:13–16 and Numbers 4:15. God specifically instructed that the ark be carried with poles on the shoulders of the Levites. But David decided on a cart. Why? Was it quicker transport? Was it safer? David runs ahead of God and trouble brews.

Uzzah and Ahio are in charge of guiding the cart with the ark of God on it. The ox pulling the cart stumbles, and the ark begins to fall off the cart. Uzzah reaches out to catch and steady the ark, and God strikes him dead (2 Samuel 6:1–11). Uzzah might have instinctively reacted without thinking, as a natural reaction to stabilize the cart. He also might have believed that it was his duty to protect God. Uzzah, as the priest, might have been trying to protect the Holy Ark by not allowing it to hit the dirty earth. Regardless of the whys, God brings swift judgment to Uzzah. Scripture does not say what made Uzzah reach out and touch the ark, but God makes it clear that His holy instructions are to be followed.

Can you identify with Uzzah? Do you attempt to protect God from the dirt of your world? From your unworthiness? Well, you don't have to. God sent His one and only Son to die for you so that you can become the heir of God's kingdom. When we have healthy walls of self-esteem, we carry ourselves the way God intended—through His instruction. We honor God by loving ourselves, properly esteeming ourselves and knowing that we were bought with a great price—the precious blood of Jesus. You and I are priceless!

Now back to King David: David was terrified of God's judgment and decides to leave the ark in the house of Obed-Edom, the Gittite. The ark was there for three months. God blessed Obed-Edom and his entire household (2 Samuel 6: 9–11). Once again, David decides to go back and get the ark. This time I believe he does so with a different attitude. He now shows honor by sacrificing a bull and a fattened calf. He goes rejoicing. What I love most about this point in the story is that David is dancing mightily before the Lord. He is worshipping in spirit and truth. He is leaping and dancing half-naked as he enters the city of David. David recognized that he needed God. It was God who had cared for him throughout his whole life, and so David rejoiced with all his might in celebration before God. (2 Samuel 6:12–15).

David did not care what anyone else thought except God. He wasn't looking around to compare himself with, if, or how others were dancing. He just danced, in his own way, without caring about anyone's thoughts of him. That is exactly how we need to respond to God's call of love; with a reckless dance and worship as if no one is watching (even when they are). We need to know whose we are. Once we do, we will not have a care about what others think of us. As long as we are right with God, we can have healthy walls of esteem and dance with reckless abandon before Him, without worrying about someone else's opinion.

What would make you dance before the Lord, with all your might and without a care for what others thought? The truth is, we should dance before the Lord each day, no matter what someone's opinion is about us. We should worship each moment we get.

I was at a funeral to support my friend, whose niece, Brittany, had died. She was in her twenties, and was brutally murdered. At the memorial, a friend got up to share a tribute to Brittany. She told us that Brittany was an encourager. Shortly before she died, Brittany had texted her to encourage her because she was going through a rough spot in her life. Her friend continued to tell us that she texted Brittany back and said she did not understand the senseless things that were happening in her life. Then Brittany replied, "It is not my job to make sense of things. It is my job to laugh and dance until I fall down and then get up and laugh and dance."

Oh how I long to live out what Brittany preached to her friend. I want to laugh and dance through my days in a spectacular show of worship. It is when we highly esteem ourselves that we are able do this. When we recognize our ultimate need for God and His approval alone, then we can worship, dance and love with reckless abandon, without a care of what others think.

Let's return to the story of David, and examine Michal, who was David's wife and the daughter of Saul. We pick up in 2 Samuel 6: 16, as Michal is watching David and the crowd come dancing into town. "And when she saw King David leaping and dancing before the Lord, she despised him in her heart" (v.16). I can just visualize her, the royal Michal watching from a distance and growing angry. Can you hear her mumble under her breath, *How dare my husband act so foolishly before the people who serve him?* Anger builds, and she is ready to blast David when he walks through the door.

She was worried about what others thought. What would people think of the king for acting this way and what will they think of her? Shouldn't David act more proper like her father, King Saul? How many times have we been embarrassed by other's actions? By being embarrassed, we are indeed worried about what others think.

I went to dinner with some friends. One of the ladies with us began to talk loudly and laugh, and really get into the conversation. One of her close friends attempted to quiet her, and seemed embarrassed that her friend was happier and louder than normal. It was interesting to watch her friend turn on her—if you will. Her friend looked at me and rolled her eyes as if to say, "I don't know this person and I am not associated with her." But what in turn happened was that I lost a bit of respect for the denying friend. She was too worried about what others were thinking. She was worried that, because of her friend's actions, she would be thought less *cool* or *less popular.* This stems from unhealthy walls of self-esteem. It is not wrong to correct your friend for being loud, but when one shuns for fear of what others think, it reveals one's true insecurities.

Michal was also worried about what others thought of her. Instead of running out to meet her husband and join in the celebration, she decided to wait and react with bitterness in her heart. When Michal meets David just outside the front door, she calls him vulgar. David responds in verse 21, that "It was before the Lord." So David is saying, "I don't care what you think. When I am dancing unto the Lord, His thoughts are the only ones that count." Ouch, Michal!

David continues to tell her he will become even more undignified than this. "So take that, woman!" Can you hear him? I love his confidence. I love how he only worries about what God thinks and no one else. He worships the way we need to worship. We were created to worship—that is what we are meant to do.

How is your worship unto the Lord? Do you worship in spirit and truth without a care of what others think? Not just in church, but do you worship with all your might, each moment you live? Can you laugh and dance until you fall down, and then get up and laugh and dance?

One day in church, I had the privilege to sit next to a young lady with Down's syndrome. She sang all the worship songs really loudly and out of tune. She raised her hands in reverence to God. Free, reckless, and not caring what others thought. Oh, to be so in love with Jesus. To sing and worship with all our might before the Lord like her, without caring one iota what ANYONE thinks.

Healthy walls of esteem grow into place when you have confidence in who you are and know *whose* you are. Confidence is not based on feelings or good days and bad days. It is something that is imbedded within you and you know that you are something special in His eyes—PERIOD!

CORRECT SELF-TALK

When my husband and I first got married, I was surprised by his words. Every day he would tell me that I was beautiful or compliment me somehow. He has continued to do this for twenty-five years! The way I feel about myself today is totally different than I did twenty-five years ago. When I was in my twenties, I had much less self-esteem than I do today. Some of that comes through experience, but his words have had an incredible impact on my life.

Words are important. Correct self-talk is just as important; reminding yourself of your gifts and talents helps combat negative thoughts and words.

Author Lauren Miller suggests that we should get our thinking and words in alignment. In order to do this, when we have a negative thought, we should think the positive while saying it out loud. For example, when we think we are not beautiful, we immediately think the opposite while saying, "I am beautiful. I am worthy. I am loved." Try doing this when you are feeling down about yourself.

The Jericho Girls did this for a month, and we all agreed that it worked. We did it for any negative thoughts, not just low self-esteem. Every time we had wrong thinking about anything we would think the correct thought (opposite of the negative thought we had) and confess the positive. Give it a try.

Getting our thinking in alignment with our words helps build healthy walls of self-esteem. We need to break down unhealthy walls of self-esteem because, first of all, they are not healthy for us! This is not how God designed us to live. Each of us is fearfully and wonderfully made. When we do not acknowledge that we are made just the way God hand-crafted and intended, we are telling God that His works are not wonderful. Unhealthy walls of self-esteem also keep us from others. How can we have healthy friendships and relationships if we are not first healthy ourselves?

Self-esteem begins in the mind, so meditate daily on what a treasure you are. Use your mess-ups to learn from, and don't beat yourself up about them. Remind yourself that you are "fearfully and wonderfully made"—imperfections and all! Practice loving yourself because God loves you, and He thinks you are precious. It is a challenge to break down the walls of unhealthy self-esteem and build healthy ones in their place. Healthy self-image begins with embracing who we are, including our perceived imperfections. As we embrace all that we are comprised of and develop correct self-talk, we can begin to quit worrying about what others think and live our lives in a dance of worship. I pray that you will have the attitude of Brittany: "It is not my job to make sense of things. It is my job to laugh and dance until I fall down and then get up and laugh and dance." Get up, laugh, and dance, beautiful woman of God.

"You can't dance with God if you're even one step ahead of Him or one step behind Him. You'll be stepping all over His feet—very messy! But, when you stay in the moment and let God lead, then you flow across the dance floor and the result is a thing of great beauty."
—Ann Maloney

JERICHO GIRLS' RESPONSE: CAN YOU IDENTIFY WITH THEM?

At the beginning of our Jericho Girls session on Walls of Esteem, the Jericho Girls each picked a rock, held it and studied it. We all wrote our reactions to what we saw, thought, and experienced by peering at our rocks. Here is what one Jericho Girl wrote and shared:

ROCK, OH MY ROCK

Oh my Rock, you remind me of a worry stone.

When I hold you in my hand, your coolness becomes warm.

I feel calmer being able to rub my thumb back and forth over your rough edges.

Maybe I'll be able to smooth some of the sharpness away-both from you, Oh Rock, and from my worries.

Oh my Rock, you give weight to my concerns but comfort that you Oh Rock, will probably last longer than my worries.

JERICHO GIRLS' TOOL BOX:

Pencil in time to love who you are.

"Your beauty should not come from outward adornment, such as elaborate hairstyles and the wearing of gold jewelry or fine clothes. Rather, it should be that of your inner self, the unfading beauty of a gentle and quiet spirit, which is of great worth in God's sight" (1 Peter 3:3–4).

"Be yourself; everyone else is already taken."–Oscar Wilde

TRAINING YOUR SOUL AND BREAKING DOWN WALLS:

Evaluate your worship to God. Do you need to change the way you respond to God's love so that your worship is pure and reckless for Him? Do something that makes you dance before the Lord with all your might without caring what others think of you.

7
WALLS OF MASKS

MASKS

We have all worn a mask at one time or another. Can you remember a time you wore one? Maybe it was when you were a child and you dressed up for Halloween. It might have been at a birthday party, or you might have participated in Mardi Gras and worn it as part of your costume. Wearing a mask is a great way to change your appearance or conceal your identity. As women, we attempt to change our appearance by changing our hairstyle, our makeup, and our wardrobe.

We also wear masks which are not physical. Even though they are not physical masks, they are very real. All over the world, women wear invisible masks to portray different roles. Wearing these invisible masks can give us a feeling of protection. They can enable us to speak up when we don't think we have a voice, appear more attractive, or hide behind a difficult situation. They allow us to lie. The list goes on and on.

While we can believe that a mask can help us feel safe in certain situations, in the long term, they just limit us. Masks give the illusion that we are something different than we are.

I once met a woman who was brand new to the lending industry. She was introduced at an educational seminar as "the newbie." She had a couple of choices for how she could present herself to her audience. First, she could have chosen to wear a self-assured mask to make her appear more confident in her abilities. However, she opted for her second choice; she nervously smiled at the crowd and displayed her insecurity. She looked uncertain because of her lack of experience. Would a mask have helped her, or just hidden her nervousness? Two extremes—one sitting looking nervous, and the other, wearing a mask and pretending to know everything while faking it.

She actually had a third choice. She could have highlighted both her knowledge and her confidence about the lending industry by being candid with the Realtors in the room. Then she could have let them know that if she didn't have the answer to their questions, she would find out for them. This would have been the best choice for both her and her audience.

Wearing a mask to misrepresent ourselves to others will lead to trouble when these misrepresentations are discovered. Long term, it can lead to becoming a character we were not created to be. Being who God designed us to be and being true to self is always the best choice—NOT wearing a mask.

When we wear masks, we become miserable, we trap ourselves in a false world. If we wear masks to hide who we truly are, we can become the mask. This is where it becomes dangerous. Trying to be someone you are not is not what God intended for you. If you wear a mask and are attempting to break free from it, practice taking it off one small step at a time. Take it off and allow God to bring you back to your original design. Rest from the mask. Eventually, you will find that you don't need it.

When you practice eliminating your masks and revealing the real you, walls will come down. You begin to become your true self again and can eventually be who you were designed to be. This can be easier said than done. We wear some masks so long that we don't know where the real us begins and the mask ends. Masks worn to protect us from situations that are raw and tender may seem impossible to remove. This is where a chisel comes in. These types of masks cannot simply be torn off. They need time to be chiseled off, bit-by-bit and piece-by-piece. Once we begin to do this, it is easier to finally chip away the mask that we have been held hostage to for so long. As we prayerfully work on chipping away our masks, remember that we are in the hands of a skilled, sensitive Sculptor.

For years, my husband viewed me as a 'sugar coater'. He said that I tell people what they want to hear. In contrast, I always saw him as a bull in a china shop, regarding how he spoke to others. In other words, he was truthful to the point of being hurtful. Although we were polar opposites in how we interacted with others, in reality we both wore masks. My mask enabled me to give everyone the answer they wanted so they would like me. I believe that most of the time I was truthful. The way I conveyed my answers to people was so sweet that they always left feeling good. In reality, they might have needed some truth along with grace. It can seem impossible to be totally truthful in every circumstance or situation we are faced with. Some of us crack under the pressure of wanting to look good or be right or. . . . We all fall prey to hiding behind falseness. Let me share with you a mask that I struggle to remove.

I wear a mask with some people in my family. There are things that they say to each other that are hurtful. Normal conversation in their household consistently tears each other down. They consider this type of destructive conversation to be normal. They are not bad people, but they have allowed their relationships with each other to become demeaning. In doing so, over time, it has become a part of their daily interactions with one another. The mask that I wear with them lets them believe that this is acceptable behavior. I *attempt* to tell them that what they are doing and saying is not right, but in such a *sugar coated* way that it goes unrecognized. Thus, I don't actually confront the situation. Wearing this mask enables me to attempt to give them good advice and still be loved by them, while they continue to cut down each other.

I still wear that mask today. I am working on a way to chisel it off. In this difficult situation, the best action would be to confront the matter, but I am not certain that that would produce the desired changes. The outcomes are unpredictable. Even though there is rich value in speaking the truth in love, my family members have to want to change.

See, there it is again—my mask of excuses! Why should I not confront the situation? I know what the answer is, but I have to want to change, too. The answer is that I need to set boundaries with them. I need to say, with truth and love, that I will not be a part of this type of behavior. I have been working on this slowly, and my mask is gradually being chiseled away. I am continuously working on a balance in how I say things truthfully and yet lovingly. That is all I can do, set boundaries, speak honestly to my family, and model it. Then I have to leave the rest to God. In his book, *When Christians Act like Christians,* Jeff Rosenau poses the question, "Is tolerance loving?" He states that the world's definition of tolerance is not the Biblical definition of tolerance. Jeff discusses how Jesus did not tolerate sin, but still loved the sinner. He also states that, "Love includes truth and accountability." That is exactly how I need to approach my family situation. My husband has encouraged me to confront them, but I am afraid that it will be regarded as hurtful . I've let my fear hold me hostage under a mask of *worldly tolerance.*

Jeff also states, "If the Christian responds with truth, but without love and compassion, that Christian has forgotten that he has been forgiven (2 Peter 1:3–9), and has failed to remember the grace and mercy God has extended to him." My husband, at times, can respond to others with truth, but without love and compassion. Although he has gotten much better at responding in love, he continually works on it, as do I in with speaking more truth than grace.

WHAT DO WE HIDE BEHIND?

Masks allow us to hide behind them. They afford us an option to act and speak differently than we would without them. So what do we hide behind?

We hide behind our:

- homes ✓
- jobs ✓
- spouse ✓
- food ✓
- kids ✓✓
- hobbies ✓
- emotions or lack thereof ✓✓
- fears ✓✓✓✓✓

Can you identify with any of these?

For many years, my husband worked long hours, running a successful framing business and custom home building company. He put so much of himself into his job that it became his identity. He was so wrapped up in work, success, and planning for retirement, that work became who he was. Being dedicated to work doesn't make it a bad thing. We were all created to work and be creative. At the beginning of the Bible, in Genesis 1:1, we see God creating. "In the beginning, God *created* [italics added] the heavens and earth." "So God created man in His own image, in the image of God He created him; male and female He created them" (v. 27). Before sin occurred in the garden, Adam was working (Genesis 2:15). We are created in God's image. We are created to work and create just as God does.

My husband's hard work was not, per se, a bad thing. It is when he put it before everything else—especially God—that it became his Mask, his identity. That's what made it dangerously wrong. Patrick Rothfuss in *The Name of the Wind* says, "We understand how dangerous a mask can be. We all become what we pretend to be."

My husband's mask said, "I am my work," and therefore he became his work. He identified himself through his job. My mask of dealing with my family's behavior made me become what I was pretending to be—the nice family member who simply wanted to be loved, and not confrontational. Wearing that mask makes me miserable. We need to practice being before God and being an apprentice of Jesus. We need to strip off our masks and imitate the One we were created for—in His image—not by hiding behind a mask. As we practice being more like Jesus, we will eventually become like Him. If we pretend to be something we are not and wear masks, then we will become the false person we pretend to be. Jesus wasn't fake; He was real. Not allowing ourselves to hide behind masks and practicing being more like Jesus helps us to BE more like Him. This is why we train our souls. Each training allows us to practice being a better apprentice and helps us to break down walls. It truly helps us become more like Him.

We can hide behind many things, including our homes and things we acquire that help us appear to have a certain social status. We can hide behind our jobs, identifying our worth through success. We can also hide behind a person, a spouse, for example, which allows us be identified as "married." Anyone who has gone through a divorce can attest to the social status of the label "married" versus "divorced." We can hide behind food, which masks some other emotional need. Hiding behind something translates to being fearful of something. Why do we allow "masking" in our lives? Because it is easy—easier to hide than confront whatever keeps us frozen behind our fears.

WHAT ARE WE AFRAID OF?

We are all afraid of something. We might have been hurt by someone and are afraid of getting hurt again. We might have low self-esteem that makes us afraid to speak up or offer an opinion. We can be afraid of being without—whether that is without a loved one, without a job, money and possessions, without our health, without our homes, or without friends and meaningful relationships.

What are you afraid of? Do you know that you are not alone in your fears? Wearing a mask is typically driven by some type of fear. When we give in to wearing one, it allows us to venture from behind our walls and interact with less fear. Unfortunately, we still attempt to shield ourselves with a mask instead of a wall—neither of them good options.

The Jericho Girls shared many of their fears. In giving into fear, they put on masks. A woman I know is widowed, remarried, and then divorced. When asked her marital status, she says she is widowed. She is widowed but more recently, she is divorced. She is not able to tell others that she is divorced, so she wears a mask saying she is widowed instead. Many people of the Bible were afraid too. Guess what? They wore masks. For example:

Moses was afraid to be God's spokesman (Exodus 3–4).

In Exodus 3, we read about an incredible encounter between God and man. God appears to Moses in a burning bush. God tells Moses that He has heard the cry of His people, and He is going to rescue them from their oppression in Egypt.

God instructs Moses to go to Pharaoh and bring His people out of Egypt. Moses says to God, "Who am I that I should go to Pharaoh and bring the Israelites out of Egypt?" Moses does not believe in himself. I wonder if Moses had a self-esteem issue. He continues to argue with God (see the conversation in Exodus 3 and 4:1–17).

Moses was afraid to speak to the Israelites. Ultimately, he missed out on the blessing that God had in store for him, to be God's main speaker. Instead, Aaron, Moses' brother, became God's spokesman. Moses wore a mask by hiding behind his brother, Aaron. He could not believe that God would use him to speak to the Israelites, so he hid behind his brother. Although Moses hid behind a mask, God still spoke to him. Then Moses spoke to Aaron, who was Moses' mouthpiece. God still used Moses in a mighty way.

Abraham hid behind a mask of lies (Genesis 12:11–20).

Abram tells his wife, Sarai, to say to the Egyptians that she was his sister and not his wife. Abram feared the Egyptians would see how beautiful Sarai was, kill Abram, and take Sarai for their own. Although Sarai was indeed his half-sister, she was also his wife. Abram lied by telling a half-truth. He did this not once, but twice (see also Genesis 20:1). Abraham hid behind a mask of lies and did not trust God to guide them where they were going, or trust God to protect them.

Peter was afraid for his life and denied Jesus (John 18:15–27).

Peter hid behind a mask of denial out of fear. The same Peter, who, shortly before his denial, proclaimed to Jesus, "Lord, why can't I follow you now? I will lay down my life for you" (John 13:37). After such a heart-felt commitment to Jesus, Peter, in fear, denied knowing Him. If Peter had confessed that he knew Jesus when Jesus was arrested, Peter might have been arrested too. His life could have been in jeopardy. I do not judge Peter. I have worn a mask of denial for much more trivial reasons. After all, Peter's life was at risk – but still, he hid.

Joshua was scared (Joshua 1:1–9).

After Moses' death, Joshua was scared and intimidated by the weight of responsibility he had assumed as Moses' successor. God spoke to him and assured him that there was no need to be afraid, since God was with him. Joshua hid behind a mask of insecurity. Who wouldn't feel insecure attempting to walk in Moses' footsteps? But unlike Moses, Joshua obeyed the call of God. He removed the mask and simply obeyed.

Queen Esther wore a mask of deception (Esther 5).

Esther held a banquet for her husband, the King, and for Haman, his right hand man. She intended to reveal to the King the true nature of Haman, who was plotting to destroy the Jews. While wearing her mask of deception, she asks the King to come to a banquet she has prepared for him and Haman. It is there that she reveals to the King Haman's true motives. Even though Queen Esther's motives were right in saving the Jewish people, she still wore a mask of deception.

Isaiah wore a mask of shame and guilt (Isaiah 6).

He thought he was too sinful. Isaiah saw the Lord in His Glory and then saw himself in all his uncleanness. How could Isaiah *not* feel shame, seeing himself revealed in the presence of the Holy One? He was also scared to death, because anyone who saw God expected to die immediately. Isaiah was then cleansed, his guilt and sin was atoned for.

Judas wore a mask of deception when he betrayed Jesus.

Who else can you think of that wore masks in the bible? Isn't it wonderful to read that God blessed these people in the Bible even though they wore masks? Imagine the blessing if we were maskless.

Do you know who never wore a mask? Jesus.

Jesus wept. He was never afraid of showing His emotions. He didn't put on a "tough guy" mask. Jesus wept over the death of Lazarus (John 11:35); He wept over Jerusalem (Luke 19:41); and Jesus wept tears of anguish in the garden (Luke 22:39–46 and Hebrews 5:7).

Jesus clears the temple. He gets mad in the temple and shows his emotions (John 2:12–22).

Jesus tells it like it is to the Pharisees, to the woman at the well, and to so many others. Jesus never wore a mask. He was REAL.

APPEALING TO WHOM?

Have you ever known someone but never really knew who they truly were? Knowing someone only on the surface leaves a distance, a void between two people in a relationship. How can you really love someone you do not truly know? Whether with a friend or in an intimate relationship, you need to know the person before you can really know and love who they are.

One of my best friends had a difficult time letting people truly know her. When I first met her, I wanted to get to know her better, but she had a huge wall around her heart and she dare not let anyone look over that wall. She had been hurt many times, and she was done sharing her heart with everyone. As our friendship grew and trust was built, she slowly tested the waters, letting me see more of who she was. When she realized that I loved what I saw, she continued to let me get closer and get to know her better.

I have known her for many years, but it has been only in the last three years that I have been able to really know her more deeply. She is like a sister to me now, but this relationship has been years in the making. I don't think she has totally let her guard down with me, but we have made huge progress over the years. I love being with her. What she did not realize was that hiding behind her mask, did not make her appealing. It was the glimpses of the real her, that made her enchanting. In reality, her "tough girl" mask that she thought would protect her, made her less attractive. Only a friend can see behind the falseness and want to love the real you. Hiding behind a mask isn't pretty, because it's not the real you.

Reflect

Do you know who else wants to see the real you? God. He already knows who you really are. We can pretend to hide from God but He created us and He knows everything about us. Psalm 139:13–14 says:

> For you created my inmost being; you knit me together in my mother's womb. I praise you because I am fearfully and wonderfully made; your works are wonderful, I know that full well.

God even knows how many strands of hair you have (Luke 12:7):

> Indeed, the very hairs of your head are all numbered. Don't be afraid; you are worth more than many sparrows.

God wants us to be like His Son, and His Son never wore a mask. Jesus was real. Stop "masking" and living roles that aren't truly you. This is difficult because masks feel safe. A mask will not protect you, nor will it allow you to be who God intended you to be. We need to begin to take off our masks and accept who we are. All of our good and bad experiences shape who we are, so unmask and share the real you.

God welcomes our honesty. God is saying, "Show me the person that you are." Sometimes we are ashamed to be ourselves before others and God. Sometimes what we need most is to accept ourselves as we really are. We may need to change. In either case, as we see in Psalm

51, honesty is the place to begin: "The sacrifice acceptable to God is a broken spirit, a broken and contrite heart, O God, you will not despise."

"This too, is a small surrender, when we drop our masks and disguises and present ourselves authentically to God. It is another kind of repentance, a way to return." Emilie Griffin, *Small Surrenders*.

Don't delay, begin today to chisel away those masks and become the authentic person God made you.

JERICHO GIRLS' RESPONSE: CAN YOU IDENTIFY WITH THEM?

- *I wore a mask very early on in my childhood—and I put on a mask to pretend things weren't happening.*

- *I am the oldest of my siblings. I had an alcoholic father and when he would come home drunk, I would help shield my brother and sisters from his verbally abusive ways. I wore a mask to enable me to do this for them.*

- *I am a fixer so I wore a fixer's mask. I am the middle child and I learned very quickly how to keep balance within the family. I would go around fixing all the household problems so that we would not have any arguments in the family.*

- *I wear different masks for different situations. They are not all bad masks. For example, I wear a mask as a business woman and a different mask in social settings. Basically, I put on a mask to fit the situation.*

- *Only two people see me 'maskless', and it is because they are 'maskless' with me.*

○ *Wearing masks is a learned behavior. We learn to wear them early in life.*

○ *It is difficult to take your mask off when someone else has theirs on.*

JERICHO GIRLS' TOOL BOX:

Chisel away those masks!

"Every word of God is flawless; He is a **shield** to those who take refuge in Him" (Proverbs 30:5, emphasis added).

TRAINING YOUR SOUL AND BREAKING DOWN WALLS:

Be aware of when you are wearing your mask(s) and when you are not. When you recognize you are hiding behind a mask, ask God to be the only shield you need. Allow someone to see a glimpse of the real you—I bet they will like what they see!

mask	Fear behind it
shyness	I won't fit in
stuck up	& I don't know how to relate to others.
quiet- freezing people out	I don't know how to talk with others about defining me—my concerns, my boundaries
anger	I can't control my kids
happiness	I fear letting others in.
Everything is fine	complaining worry

worry
negative—it I'm probably thing won't turn out good.

K will steal the kids and there is nothing God can do about it.

8

WALLS OF ISOLATION

ISOLATION

Every day, there are battles to fight: getting the kids out the door in time for school, deadlines at work, disagreements with others, freeway traffic, battling our will. We are in daily combat. But there are other battles raging around us. Spiritual battles. We need to be reminded that there is more to this life than just us. There are many things going on that we are not even aware of—spiritual things. We need to tune into the heavenly realms, watch, and be alert to what is happening before us and around us. The book of Ephesians reminds us of this: "Finally, be strong in the Lord and in His mighty power. Put on the full armor of God, so that you can take your stand against the devil's schemes. For our struggle is not against flesh and blood, but against the rulers, against the authorities, against the powers of this dark world and against the spiritual forces of evil in the heavenly realms" (Ephesians 6:10–12).

As we return to the story of Joshua, chapter 5:13–15, we see that Joshua is near Jericho. He sees what he perceives to be a man, standing in front of him with a drawn sword in his hand. Joshua goes to the man and asks, "Are you for us or for our enemies?" "Neither," he replied, "but as the commander of the army of the Lord, I have now come." Then Joshua falls face down to the ground in reverence, and asks him, "What message does my Lord have for His servant?"

Many times we fail to see the spiritual battle going on around us. At first, Joshua thought his encounter was with a man, but in reality, this being was from the heavenly realms. He was "the commander of the army of the Lord." This "man" is Christ pre-incarnate. We can conclude this because of Joshua's response; he fell facedown to the ground in reverence, and was allowed to do so. The only person who is allowed to be worshiped is God. In other scriptures such as Revelation 19:10, John is scolded for falling down in worship because he fell down before an angel. "At this I fell at his feet to worship him. But he said, 'Don't do that! I am only a fellow servant with you and with your brothers and sisters who hold to the testimony of Jesus. Worship God! For it is the Spirit of prophecy who bears testimony to Jesus.' "

Joshua is also instructed to take off his sandals because the place he is standing is "holy"—just like Moses' encounter with God at the burning bush.

We see that, even though at first glance Joshua thought he saw a man, when he spoke to this person, he immediately realized he was of the spiritual realm. Joshua quickly "tuned in" to spiritual things. No wonder he was selected to be the new leader to guide God's people, the Israelites, after Moses died. As children of God's chosen people, we too, are commanded to be tuned in to spiritual things.

One of the spiritual things we need to be cognizant of is bringing down walls that hinder us from seeing spiritually. One of the major walls that blocks our spiritual vision is the wall of isolation. Isolation hides us from God and from relationships. Satan is the master of keeping us isolated. When Satan is successful at keeping us away from God and our godly sisters, depression can set in and result in despair, loss of hope, fear, self-absorption, and loss of perspective.

Walls of isolation are one of the worst walls we can build around our hearts. When we hide in isolation, the first thing that can happen is that we distance ourselves from God and from others. When we distance our hearts and unplug from relationships, we can quickly lose perspective. This happens slowly at first, subtly. Before we know it, we lose our desire to pray and to be with our godly friends. When we are not praying and staying in tune with spiritual things, our faith fades. Pushing others away keeps us from the very ones who could help us get back on track and correct and guide us. Before you know it, we spiral into the next phase: self-pity, depression, and despair. From there, fears build in our hearts. Without others to help us sort out true and false fears, to aid in sorting out correct thinking, what we think we can and cannot handle, we quickly become more isolated.

So what is the antidote? Break down those walls fast! Reach out to others, even when we do not *feel* like it. Pray, read our Bibles, and practice spiritual disciplines such as breath prayer.

Sometimes that is the only thing left within us—to practice breath prayer. Maybe all we can do is inhale and exhale calling the name of Jesus. Breath prayer is reciting a short scripture or statement to Jesus by saying the first part while inhaling and saying the second part while exhaling. Sometimes that is the only thing we have—whispering the name of Jesus or a short scripture we know. As we continue to call upon His name, the prayers flow more readily and before we know it, we are spending more and more time in His presence.

Whatever one can muster up to do, something needs to be done. Sometimes this means getting professional help.

When we are in this place of isolation, wallowing is easier than pushing through. As God's warriors, we are called to battle. We need to fight, kick, and shout at these walls until they come tumbling down. God created us for relationship and that is how we are hard-wired.

When we isolate ourselves, we go against our encoded nature, which is unhealthy. No matter what you have to do, dear warrior, get out from behind the walls of isolation.

One of my favorite reads on spiritual battles is C.S. Lewis' *The Screw Tape Letters*. The story takes place following a sequence of letters written by a senior demon, Screwtape, to his nephew, Wormwood, a demon in training. Uncle Screwtape is instructing his protégé on how to win the soul of a British man, referred to as, "the patient". The book walks us through an average man's life, with all its temptations as seen and provoked from Satan's perspective. It is a brilliant read to open the mind to spiritual "happenings" within our world. It reminds us that Satan will do whatever he can to destroy us. He wants us isolated because once we are in isolation, we are easy prey. God's warriors can combat evil because Jesus has already won the battle for us! Because He has already won, we are able to battle both the physical and spiritual, each moment of our lives.

> *Be on guard against the pit of self-pity. When you are weary or unwell, this demonic trap is the greatest danger you face. Don't even go near the edge of the pit. Its edges crumble easily, and before you know it, you are on the way down. It is ever so much harder to get out of the pit than to keep a safe distance from it. That is why I tell you to be on guard. There are several ways to protect yourself from self-pity. When you are occupied with praising and thanking Me, it is impossible to feel sorry for yourself. Also, the closer you live to Me, the more distance there is between you and the pit. Live in the light of my presence by fixing your eyes on Me. Then you will be able to run with endurance the race that is set before you, without stumbling or falling. (Jesus Calling, Sara Young, February 23.)*

So how do we stay away from this 'pit' that Sara Young describes? We start with just a small prayer. Sometimes that is all we can muster up. We also need to return to fellowship. Without fellowship, we again find ourselves in isolation headed back toward the 'pit'. Our sisters in Christ help us to see spiritually. They turn us around and lead us back to Christ. Both a return to God and surrounding ourselves with our sisters are ways to break walls that block our spiritual vision. Once this wall is removed, we are open and ready to see things through the eyes of God and are able to see and deal with the spiritual and physical happenings around us. ·

GOOD WALLS

WALLS OF PROMISE

Now the gates of Jericho were securely barred because of the Israelites. No one went out and no one came in. Then the LORD said to Joshua, "See, I have delivered Jericho into your hands, along with its king and its fighting men. March around the city once with all the armed men. Do this for six days. Have seven priests carry trumpets of rams' horns in front of the ark. On the seventh day, march around the city seven times, with the priests blowing the trumpets. When you hear them sound a long blast on the trumpets, have the whole army give a loud shout; then the wall of the city will collapse and the army will go up, everyone straight in" (Joshua 6:1–5).

God promised Joshua that Jericho would be delivered into his hands. God was with him in his battle against the Canaanites. Joshua's response was one of obedience. Sometimes we miss the promises of God because we don't follow in obedience. Why? We all want the promises of God. We all want the blessings to flow. It is because we need to erect a wall of promise around our hearts. When we remember what God promises, we don't lose our perspective. With correct perspective, we are free from the bondage of isolation. When we memorize the word of God and speak it, it breathes truth into our lives. Joshua was instructed to do so: "Keep this Book of the Law always on your lips; meditate on it day and night, so that you may be careful to do everything written in it. Then you will be prosperous and successful" (Joshua 1:8).

We so easily look at our situations and lose hope. If we allow this to continue, we can begin to isolate our hearts. We lose sight of the One who is in charge of our battles. Erecting healthy, God given walls of promise that protect us from the enemy and loneliness is what keeps the embers of our hearts aflame. This, in turn, leads us to obedience. Obedience is where we find blessing. We need walls of promise surrounding our hearts to guard us and keep us focused on God. Walls of promise provide hope and reassurance that God, the Commander of the Army, is with us and for us.

When God makes a promise to us, we can be assured that He will keep it. But sometimes we lose heart, because it is not happening in the time frame that we expect. I have a friend who has been obedient to God for a very long time, and still has not received the promise.

She is discouraged and is left wondering when He will remember His promise to her.

She wonders why it is taking so long. The last thing my friend wants to hear right now is that God's timing is perfect. She knows this, but she is weary from waiting. In times like these, we need to stay focused. We need to remember that God is not bound to time—He is timeless. He is, He was, and He will always be. Time can be a tyrant. My friend needs to push through, continuing to write the promise on her heart, and utilize the minutes of her life while she is waiting. Serving others is a great way to utilize your time while waiting. What happens, is that your perspective shifts from you to another person. Isn't that how Jesus spent His time, serving others?

Are you a weary warrior? Continue to write the promises of God on your heart. Build healthy walls of promise, even when you do not see the promise coming. What we forget is that when we read the scriptures, we read a story from beginning to the end. We see the promise but tend to forget that many times, the person in the story had to wait on God's promises. Remember that in your life too. God never takes back His promise. It might not arrive in the time you expect or in the way you expect. Stand up, Warrior, you are stronger than you think you are.

ARMED GUARDS AND REAR GUARDS

In Joshua 6:6–11, Joshua calls a meeting with the priests and gives them the instruction that the LORD gave to him. He instructs them to have armed guards go ahead of the ark and rear guards follow the procession. First, we need to define what a guard is.

Dictionary.com defines the verb "to guard" as:

1. *to keep safe from harm or danger; protect; watch over: to guard the ruler*

2. *to keep under close watch in order to prevent escape, misconduct, etc.: to guard a prisoner*

3. *to keep under control or restraint as a matter of caution or prudence: to guard one's temper*

4. *to provide or equip with some safeguard or protective appliance, as to prevent loss, injury, etc.*

Therefore, an armed guard would be one who carries some type of weapon to protect and guard the item or person which they are guarding. The Israelites marched around the city walls of Jericho once a day for six days. They carried the ark and had armed guards in the front, the priest following next with their trumpets, with the ark and the rear guards following the procession.

What an eerie sight this must have been when the Canaanites watched as God's chosen people marched in silence. The only sound heard was the sound of the ram's horn. Front armed guards are the first to reach the battle lines therefore, the front guards functioned as the main protectors. However, the rear guards were no less important. They made up the final contingents of the army and protected the Israelites 'backs'.

Who has God placed in your life as "armed guards" in front to guide, mentor and be an encourager in your life? Who has God placed in your life as "rear guards" who has got your back and pushes you out of your comfort zone? Everyone needs people like this in their lives. Identify them and allow them to help you.

THE SEVENTH DAY

Why was the seventh day so important in this scenario? For six days previous, God's people did exactly what was asked of them. They marched around the walls of Jericho in silence and returned to camp as instructed. They were obedient. They followed God's instruction, even when it made no sense at all. "March around the walls, God? Really? How is this supposed to knock down the walls of Jericho?"

They did not ask why, they did not complain. Despite the ridicule of the Canaanite people, who probably thought they were off their rocker, they continued to march—just as God instructed. They took God at His word, even when it did not make sense.

Some speculate that because the Israelites had a history of complaining and grumbling, this was the very reason that God said to march in silence. Ultimately, whether there was internal grumbling or not, they followed His instruction.

Many times, we fail to march—we fail to move forward and then walls of isolation build. We get stuck. When we get stuck, we fail to receive God's promises because, many times, we are not obedient to His word. When we fail to follow God's instruction, we don't see the promise. Sometimes we follow the instruction and still fail to see the promise. The Israelites followed the instruction for six days. They were not seeing the promise. Do you suppose they got weary and wondered, "When will these walls come down? What if we got the instruction wrong?" I suppose they had doubts too. Especially when what was asked of them seemed impossible. Marching around a HUGE wall in silence. "Joshua, are you sure you got the instructions from the LORD correct?" Six long days of marching brought no result. But we see in verses 15–21 that the seventh day was different. On the seventh day, Joshua instructed them to march around the walls seven times. On the seventh time around, when the priest sounded the trumpet blast, Joshua commanded the people to "Shout!" When the trumpets sounded, the people shouted and the walls came crumbling down. God did it! He came through. Oh, what a glorious moment for the Israelites. They received God's promise.

When we continue to write the promises of God on our hearts, not building up walls of isolation but forcing ourselves to march forward, even when the circumstances appear impossible, it is then when we see the impossible in our lives become possible. Of course, this is always in God's perfect timing—the "seventh day".

What is the main, unhealthy wall that you hold tight around your heart that needs to come crumbling down in your life right now? Do you see yourself moving towards isolation?

What wall of promise do you need to erect around your heart? I encourage you to stop reading at this point and get a note card and envelope. Address the envelope to yourself. Next, write a note to God answering the above question. Seal it and give it to either your front guard or rear guard. Then have them mail it to you one month from today. In one month, re-read your note card and evaluate how you have relied on God's promises to build healthy walls of promise.

Reflect on what unhealthy wall came crumbling down and how that has impacted your life. Identify how you were able to overcome isolation and how receiving help from others has helped you.

Remember, we need to walk in obedience, follow instruction and accept God's promises as true, even when we do not see the promise being fulfilled. We need to have our armed guards in place—both front and rear. Let God be your *wrecking ball,* and bring down those unhealthy walls and erect the walls of promise tightly around your heart. Let your sisters help you march through life and expect to see the seventh day arrive.

"We mutually disclose information about ourselves on increasingly deeper levels if we want to develop an increasingly closer and more meaningful friendship." Pamela Hoover Heim-Womenschool of Ministry Leadership. From an article *Avoiding Mouth Traps.*

JERICHO GIRLS' RESPONSE: CAN YOU IDENTIFY WITH THEM?

- *I am an introvert so it is easy for me to isolate.* ✓
- *I cannot do life without my front guard.*
- *Waiting for the seventh day is so difficult.* ✓
- *First, we need to be conscious of our unhealthy walls, then we need to be persistent in our prayers to remove them.* ✓

JERICHO GIRLS' TOOL BOX:

Let God be your *wrecking ball!*

"The LORD will fight for you; you need only to be still" (Exodus 14:14).

TRAINING YOUR SOUL AND BREAKING DOWN WALLS:

Set up a meeting with each of your "armed guards"—both front and rear. Talk with them about how you envision them helping you facilitate your walk with God. Maybe you do not have front and rear guards and need some. Maybe you just need a front or a rear. If so, meet with the person(s) as above and talk with them about being one of your heart guards. Pray for your armed guards as they *march* through life with you.

9

STOP, DROP AND LISTEN!

WHO IS IN CHARGE HERE?

It was time to stop and listen. We had been knocking down so many walls that we needed a break. We needed to catch our breath. So we stopped. The Jericho Girls met and formed listening groups. What is a listening group? It can consist of two or three people who spend time listening to one another.

There is immense power in being heard. But in general, we are poor listeners. Why is it so difficult to listen? For starters, our world is a busy, noisy place. Studies have shown that there are healing powers in *truly* being heard. So, the Jericho Girls met. This time we formed groups of two and followed the instruction of our spiritual director from Southeast Christian Church. She led us on an amazing journey, which allowed us to encounter God through listening.

As we gathered together in our listening group, we began with silence for a couple of minutes. When the silence was over, one person in the group began to speak. The speaker is encouraged to speak about anything that is on their heart. In our listening group, the speaker had ten minutes to talk. This is a short time. Many listening groups allow much longer for talking time, but we had a limited amount of time.

The listener's only part was to listen and not say anything while the speaker was speaking. During this time, the listener listens to the speaker, while praying to hear what God has to say about the speaker's situation. The listener can jot down a word or two, if needed, as things come to mind. When the speaker is finished talking, return to silence. After a couple of minutes of silence the speaker invites a response. The listener gives a word from God, if any.

I sat with my partner. After our initial time of silence, we both stared at each other. Who would speak first? She pointed at me (of course). I began to tell her about my work load and feeling overwhelmed with all the things I had to get done in one day. I expressed how overloaded I was. I had homework papers to write for my women's ministry leadership class. I had Bible study lessons and Jericho Girl's meetings to prepare, more alone time with God, a husband to attend to, and a business to run. Friends to minister, family to visit—oh, and writing this book had to fit into my daily agenda too. The truth was that I was tired. I felt over-loaded and did not know where to begin digging in the heaping pile of my life's duties.

As I unloaded these things onto my listening partner, I discovered a few things. First, it was just nice to talk about my difficult schedule and things I needed to get done, without someone telling me I am taking on too much. I know that I take on too much, but that's who I am. That's what is encoded in my DNA and what makes me tick. Even though I get overwhelmed at times, the truth is I enjoy accomplishing many things. I love school and learning. I savor visiting with my friends and ministering to them. I appreciate my crazy work schedule, being pulled in different directions and figuring out how to make it all happen in one day.

As much as I flourish on the craziness and getting it all done, I thrive on alone time too. In fact, my alone time is necessary for me to be able to perform the many tasks that make up my day. I was tired, and it was nice to share that with someone, without a response from them.

What I was finding was that I just needed to express my exhaustedness **without receiving a solution.** I already knew the solution.

Secondly, I discovered it was difficult to share my feelings of inadequacy with someone else. This person knows me as someone who does all things. To reveal my weakness felt raw and vulnerable. Would she think I was weak? Would she tell me to slow down and quit taking on so much? While I was speaking to my listening partner, I realized that my wall of masks was creeping up, around my heart. What else could it be but hiding behind a mask that tells others I can do it all and never feel exhausted?

Sometimes I hesitate to share. I don't want others to feel like they cannot come to me because I have too much on my plate. We don't want others to see our weaknesses—right? But what I have learned is that transparency is what allows us to relate to others. So I continued to speak about all my daily stresses and did not let my wall of masks take over. I made a decision not to re-erect the mask and instead, be real. I shared and then exhaled. There it was—all my day's worries, stresses, and burdens held in the hands of another. What would she do with my words in her control? My time was up. Then came the next round of silence. After the silence was over, I invited my listener to give a response. She simply asked me two questions:

First she asked me, "What do you hear God calling you to do?" With that question, I realized that I was so wound up about my to-do list that I had not slowed down enough to check in with God about these matters. After all, doesn't He plan my day before my day begins? The thought occurred to me that my ultimate goal is NOT to control and fix everything and that maybe I should be checking in with Him a little more frequently. *My Kids!!!*

Secondly, she simply asked, "What do you need to lay down at the feet of Jesus? And are you able to do that?" She told me that she did not have the answer to those questions but as she was praying, those were the two questions that came to her. Immediately, I thought yes, I can lay these things down before Him. But by the time I had left the listening group, I had already picked them back up from the feet of Jesus and took off running with them in my arms.

When I truly examined my heart, I didn't want to lay any of them down. They are all good things. What if God asked me to actually get rid of some of these things? I realized that this was something I needed to do. I needed to lay my day before God and let Him decide what He wanted me to do for the day. I received the answer, without someone telling what that was. The answer came with someone listening and asking a few simple questions. This is the beauty of listening groups.

When it was my turn to be the listener in the listening group, I discovered that I am not as good at listening as I believed I was. I found myself wanting to say something, wanting to fix my partner's problem. It felt uncomfortable, even strange, to simply sit and nod my head from time to time. But by keeping the silence, I was learning that it was not up to me to fix everything. It was up to me to do my three-way listening—listening to my partner and asking God what He would say through me. When my partner was speaking, all sorts of my own ideas welled up inside of me about how to help her. As I continued in silence, there it was, that still small voice. "I love her servant's heart, but being a servant does not equate to being taken advantage of." I knew immediately that that would not have been my first response to her situation. I would have said, "Let me tell you what I would do. I would quit . . ." You get the idea. Instead, I relayed something totally different from what my natural response would be. That's all I had. All I could give her, one sentence.

It seemed strange, giving a one sentence response and not helping her 'fix' her situation. What I learned is that it's alright to leave things undone, unfinished, and not feel like I had to solve every problem in one listening session. The listening group time showed me that God can use me, give me a word for someone, if I would just be still, and stop trying to control everything. He is the one in charge of every conversation. If I would just suppress my tendencies to lead and let Him take over!

That is what I learned that night—that I am not called to fix things. All I am called to do is pray for the person I am listening to, while listening to God for His guidance and give Him the ultimate control. I also learned that there is healing in sharing. When someone can share without the other person trying to 'fix it', many times we find our own answers, and can begin to heal ourselves.

The next morning, I took all the things that were on my plate and laid them at the feet of Jesus. I didn't want to give up the things that I love doing, but I did. The question was, would *He* require me to give up any of these things? Maybe. What if I didn't like what He asked me to give up? For now, He was not asking me to give up anything except my control over these things. I was reminded I truly had false control over these things.

Sometimes, God does require us to give up things, and sometimes He doesn't. Nevertheless, He definitely wants us to give Him ultimate control over everything. God wants us to release control in *every* area of our lives.

So there it was, laid out for me—a control freak attempting to relinquish my control—who was beginning to trust in His total control. Really, what choice did I have? Ultimately, He is in charge. He is God and I am not. That is the nugget that came from my experience of my listening group. Now I stop taking control, drop to my knees and listen whenever He gives me the opportunity—most days.

WHAT DOES GOD SAY ABOUT LISTENING?

When it comes to listening, God should be the first One that we listen to. Life is busy. We need to make space in our lives to be attentive, first to God, then to others. I have been meeting with my spiritual mentor to incorporate "spiritual rhythms" in my life. This includes slowing down, seeking God throughout my day, and attentiveness. Not only attentiveness to God, but also to others.

One of the biggest obstacles I face right now is being present. With so many things to do in the day, if I allow myself the space to stop, I feel like I lose momentum. If I lose momentum, how will I ever gear back up to get my to-do list done? What I have found is that, when I do incorporate an attentive rhythm in my life, I enjoy the moment more. I am a better listener and ultimately, I am present both to the person I am speaking with and to God.

When I am present before God, I see things I might have missed. I am in tune to that still small voice that otherwise may have been unheard in the noise of the world. When I am in the presence of others, I become a better listener and therefore can decipher God's word (if any) for that person. James 1:19 says,

> *My dear brothers, take note of this: Everyone should be quick to listen, slow to speak and slow to become angry.*

What we typically do is the opposite; we are quick to speak, slow to listen (if we listen at all) and are easily angered and annoyed.

So what do we do to be better listeners? One of the Jericho Girls suggested that we become more conscious of what we are thinking about. First, we need to hone in on what is distracting us, and then take note of where our mind is wandering to. Once we capture those thoughts, we can identify what is keeping us prisoner from being attentive.

Next, we need to be in prayer about being present in the moment and being a better listener. We miss so many things when we are not in the present. Simply put, we miss the beauty of the moment. A breathtaking sunset, a deer crossing the road, a shared moment with a trusted friend—all moments missed when we are distracted and not fully present.

Finally, we need to practice not just listening, but hearing, truly hearing. Being heard carries so much healing power. So, like me, you may need to stop what you are doing, drop all the things that you think are important, and listen. Allow yourself to hear God and others, being fully present, capturing the essence of each moment. Don't miss out on moments to listen. There is healing in being heard. Simply taking the time to listen and be heard results in bringing down walls for others and for you. Walls will begin to come down because there is power in sharing and truly being understood.

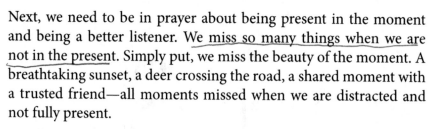

> *God has given us two ears, but one tongue, to show that we should be swift to hear, but slow to speak. God has set a double fence before the tongue, the teeth and the lips, to teach us to be wary that we offend not with our tongue.* —Thomas Watson

Jericho Girls' Response: Can you identify with them?

- *Think about what you are thinking about.*

- *I always want to fix things in conversations. I have never completely stopped and just tuned into God to hear what He has to say about the situation.*

- *I heard from God in such an amazing way by simply praying while listening.*

Jericho Girls' Tool Box:

Sand and smooth those walls that have come crumbling down.

"Be still and know that I am God" (Psalm 46:10).

Training Your Soul and Breaking Down Walls:

Practice "three-way" listening—you, the person speaking, and God. Incorporate praying while listening to the person speaking to you. Really hear that person, while listening for the still small voice, the whisper you know to be His. Push back your own thoughts and ideas and allow room for God's Word and wisdom to fill you, so that you are able to be used in a mighty way.

10

WALLS OF RESENTMENT AND FEAR

Resentment is a difficult wall to overcome. Walls of resentment have deep layers. Many times we don't acknowledge their existence, mostly because they bear our deepest hurts within their rebar (inner) structure. We need powerful tools to demolish these protective barriers. The first step is to acknowledge that these false protective walls exist. They are difficult to acknowledge; because if we do acknowledge them, we have to deal with them. It is much easier to leave these walls in place than to effect change, which can be painful.

RESENTMENT

Resentment is defined by Dictionary.com as: *the feeling of displeasure or indignation at some act, remark, person, etc., regarded as causing injury or insult*. It is said that the definition of bitterness, a companion term, is "swallowing poison and expecting another person to die." It is easy to see how unhealthy walls of resentment can be.

What causes resentment? Typically, we resent a person when we have been hurt or perceive that we have been treated poorly or unfairly. I have a friend who suffers from health issues. She has not been diagnosed with a medical condition, yet. Six years ago she began to experience unexplained seizure-like activity. Various doctors have labeled her with many diagnoses. Her ongoing diagnoses include: low blood sugar, hormonal problems, endometriosis, migraines, and MS. Yet, no one has figured out the cause of her seizures.

It has been a long six years for my friend. Each day she wakes up not feeling well, but she has to work and perform her daily personal duties of a mother, wife and friend. She has ongoing seizure episodes. She can't identify what triggers them or predict when they might occur. Each day, she puts on a smile and pretends she feels normal as she leads her coworkers for the day. At the end of the day, she comes home feeling worse; then she switches her hat to being a mom, a wife, and doing her daily chores. After all this, she collapses into bed.

I don't know how she does it—day in and day out feeling worn down, while something is going awry in her body. It's been six long years of feeling this way, going to several specialists, with various diagnoses and no favorable outcome. She has been building walls of resentment. Walls of resentment with God—which she has overcome; and walls of resentment with the doctors—who have no answers. She has walls of resentment towards her friends—who cannot possibly imagine her daily struggle. And, most recently, walls of resentment towards her husband. Let me preface with this: her husband loves her. But he, too, is frustrated with the situation.

To heap more onto their plate, they have a son who was born with a medical condition. They have spent many years caring for him. He has had many brain surgeries, and they have accumulated extremely high debt for his medical care. After all those stressful years caring for their son, there came a short hiatus before my friend began to experience her own health issues. To say the least, this family has gone through a lot!

For the past few years, her husband has been emotionally ill-equipped to deal with her health issues. He makes comments like, "Now what?" to her, when she explains she is not feeling well. Unfortunately, he simply does not know how to cope with the situation, and has said hurtful things to her. This has caused her to build walls of resentment towards him. Her resentment has also become entwined with fear. Fear that her resentment will continue to grow. She has made attempts in the past to discuss the problem with him, but to no avail. Not only does she have walls of resentment, she has fear of future hurts from him.

GET TO THE ROOT OF THE PROBLEM

Once walls of resentment are in place, it is difficult to see beyond them. Scaling them is not sufficient. We need extreme tools to break these walls down. Where do we begin? We need to begin at the foot of the wall. Typically, there is another emotion that is embedded in the base of this wall. Many times, this base is tangled, knotted, and matted with fear.

My friend has a wall of resentment rooted in fear. She is fearful that if she dissembles her resentment walls towards her husband, once her guard is down, he will continue to use hurtful words against her. She would rather keep the wall of resentment in place to prevent getting hurt. But the truth is, she is still getting hurt every time he speaks unkindly to her—even with that wall in place.

What good is that wall anyway? The wall of resentment only further isolates her and hardens her heart towards him. The wall is harmful to her. The real answer is to address her fear, address her husband, and become vulnerable—oh so frightening! My friend's defense is to shut down, hide behind her wall of resentment, and ignore her husband's words.

As God's warriors, we are called to stand for what is right, honorable, and true. We are also called to forgive repeatedly, no matter how often the offense; but we are never called to be abused. The answer lies in my friend, not her circumstances. The way she chooses to respond to her husband is what determines if the wall goes up or comes down. When unkind words from another come hurling towards our hearts, rather than hide behind a wall, we can put on God's armor.

We can let the person know that their behavior is unacceptable and what our expectations are of that person—including the expectation to be treated with respect. This is called setting boundaries. Typically, people who hurt have been hurt. Nevertheless, we can speak truth and life-giving words into their life and choose to forgive the person who hurts us. This is simply being true to ourself as God's warrior. If bad behavior from another continues, we need to be prayerful about what to do. Sometimes it means we should seek help from a counselor or mentor.

In his book, *Boundaries*, Henry Cloud states,

> *Why is avoidance a boundary problem? At the heart of the struggle is a confusion of boundaries as walls. Boundaries are supposed to be able to "breathe," to be like fences with a gate that can let the good in and the bad out. Individuals with walls for boundaries can let in neither bad nor good. No one touches them. God designed our personal boundaries to have gates. We should have the freedom to enjoy safe relationships and to avoid destructive ones. God even allows us the freedom to let Him in or to close him off, e.g., 'Here I am! I stand at the door and knock. If anyone hears my voice and opens the door, I will come in and eat with that person, and they with me' (Rev. 3:20).*

We have a choice! We can choose to set boundaries with others, letting in the good and keeping out the bad. Or we can choose to build walls that isolate us and cause bitterness. The choice is ours. We cannot simply correct or change a bad behavior. We need to identify the source behind the behavior. What is truly the origin of our resentment? Once we acknowledge the origin, then we can recognize what is driving our resentment and begin the process of breaking down walls.

Even as I write this, I identify resentment and fears in my own life that I need to deal with. Though they may seem small, that is exactly where I need to meet them—when they are small, so that they don't grow bigger. If I am lashing out at others, typically I am fearful of something in my life. If I find myself dealing with emotions of jealousy, I am admitting—if only to myself—that I am fearful of not being good enough or am comparing myself to others. Should I find myself attempting to control everything, I am typically fearful of loss.

FEAR IS AT THE ROOT OF ALL OF OUR WALLS

We are all fearful of something. As a response to that fear, we build walls. If I cannot identify who I am, I might be fearful of whom I have become. If I cannot get real with God, I may be fearful of God's response to me. I could fear being real with others because they might not like what they see. I am fearful of being hurt, so I build walls to protect my heart. If I lack self-esteem, I could be fearful of being strong and courageous. If I hide behind a mask, I could be fearful of showing the true me. If I cannot listen, I might be fearful of what truth might be spoken. **Fear drives us to build our walls.**

I have daily fears that I need to disassemble the minute they creep up on me. For example, the fear of not being in control, which is a deceptive fear. I am really not in control anyway— God is. The fear of old age and loss of independence, the fearful thought of life without my husband and being alone, the fear of not making enough money. The fears that hold us tightly in their grasp are wide and varied.

Every day, I choose life or death. I can choose to focus on my fear and I can choose to build my wall of resentment, thus choosing death and isolating my heart. When I make the decision to build walls of resentment, I swallow that pill of bitterness, and it poisons *me*—not anyone else. When I choose to accept fear in my life, it robs me of the peace God intends to give me. When I refuse to allow these walls to build and instead deal with them immediately, I empower myself to be the person God has called me to be. I choose life. That is what God tells us to do. Speaking to the Israelites when they were about to enter the Promised Land, God's spokesman Moses admonishes, "This day I call the heavens and the earth as witnesses against you that I have set before you life and death, blessings and curses. *Now choose life,* so that you and your children may live" (Deuteronomy 30:19, italics added). Obedience to God's Law was how the Israelites chose life, and still is. The benefits of choosing life spilled over to their children. By extension, when we choose life, others in our sphere of influence are blessed as well.

In her blog, Ann Voskamp says that fear and safety always turn out to be a mirage:

> He commanded it: "Do not be afraid." Go ahead, let your courage be as big as Christ is. Climb right over your fears. All He's promised you is just on the other side of fear. Because really? All fear is but the notion that God's love ends. When does He ever end? And, we've only got so much time, so let's just decide: we're done with the myth of safety. Safety's just the mirage of the living dead. Do you really want to live or not? Do a dangerous thing every day. The only way to ever find the Comfort is outside of your comfort zones-no wonder being safe leaves you restless. Do it already!

How true—rarely do our fears ever become a reality. We spend time worrying about the what-if's and wasting precious time. We tend to live in the *mirage* of our fears and play it safe. Typically, fears do not protect us. However, knowledge reduces our restrictions and enlarges our options. We have an internal mechanism called fight or flight. The fight or flight response is our body's automatic, inborn response that prepares the body to *fight* or *flee* from perceived attack, harm, or threat to our survival. This God-designed response is in place to protect us. Before we experience a "fight or flight" situation, there is another mechanism that tells us when things do not seem right or safe, that feeling that something just doesn't "feel right". Many of us have experienced this sensation of *intuition* that alerts us to when something seems unsettling. It is this inner intuition that alerts us to perceived threats or unsafe situations. For example, I might have a fear to scuba dive, but I probably will not die diving because I have prepared and practiced the necessary skills. I do not begin diving without training. Once I have mastered the skills, I can proceed with this adventure with confidence. If, on the other hand, I have an unusual feeling about a situation, I need to listen to my internal regulator. If it alerts me not to do something that particular day, then I need to obey that intuition. When I am in tune to my inner alarm, I am more apt to be guided by God's safety about the things that I do. Knowledge provides a door in the wall of fear.

God has called us to do more than hide behind walls, attempting to play life safely. He has called us to be warriors, which means pulling out the sword of truth, wearing His breastplate of righteousness, bringing down walls of resentment and fear, and living life to the fullest—having the ride of our lives!

ACKNOWLEDGING TRUE AND FALSE PERCEIVED FEARS

We all live with fear to some degree. It is what we do with those fears that can shape us for better or for worse. When I think of fearful people, a few people come to mind, including myself. Some live in a state of constant fear. Not just a normal fear, but a debilitating fear that dominates their entire day. Others are able to deal with their fears and place them in their proper perspective. Some of these fears seem small, while others are larger. But what typically happens is that a small fear can begin to grow into a cancerous, healthy cell eating disease that becomes a greater fear in the mind than it actually is.

One woman I know has a fear of being alone. She fears that if she is alone, something might happen to her and no one will be there to help her. Therefore, she constantly lets others know that she needs people around her at all times, even if it is a stranger. She wants to know that someone is there with her should she pass out, need to talk, or whatever else she could imagine happening.

As her fear has developed over the years, it has evolved in her mind to the point where it is almost impossible for her to consider being alone. She lives her life telling herself that she needs people all the time and cannot be alone. She continually confesses her fear. She will make statements like, "Give me people and I am fine. Just don't put me alone or I will freak out." But what she is doing is giving into her fear, and thus it grows in her mind.

Acknowledging a fear and feeding a fear are two different things. This woman is feeding her fear day-in and day-out. She has a perceived fear. She has not been able to overcome this fear, because she constantly speaks untruths to her heart. The truth is she does not need other people around her at all times. She needs to evaluate the reality of her what-ifs. She needs to ask herself, "What if I pass out and I am all by myself? What would happen? Well, I would probably wake up after the episode or I would wake up in the arms of Jesus, neither of them bad outcomes right? What if I need to talk to someone, and there is no one in sight? Do I panic or talk to Jesus?"

Instead, she continues to look at the fear or imagined scenario. She continues to become more fearful daily. She robs herself of peace in her day and steals the joy and beauty of her alone time with God and herself.

Another woman speaks of having the fear of driving on the freeway. This woman used to drive on the freeway all the time, but she had an incident where she took the wrong exit and could not find her way back to where she was going. She eventually found her way, but she allowed this experience to so envelop her mind that her fear grew. She continues to feed it. Today, she is terrified to drive on the freeway.

Acknowledging our fear, whether true or false, is just the beginning. The next step is to do something about it, to starve your fear. As we take a look at starving our fears, remember that if we only acknowledge our fears but we do nothing to overcome them, we are no better off. We become wrapped in fear, spending our days in worry. God has called us to be *warriors,* not *worriers.*

STARVE YOUR FEAR

After acknowledging what we fear, the next step is to stop it dead in its tracks. We need to stop fear where it begins—in the mind. When we spend time focusing on our fear and all the "what if" scenarios, we feed the fear. As we feed the fear, it becomes bigger and bigger. We need to do the opposite. We need to become bigger than the fear. The ability to become big over the fear means that we need to be in charge of it. When we let our minds race with ideas and possibilities that *potentially* could happen, we allow fear to control us. On the other hand, when we take charge of our minds, refusing to let thoughts of fear rule, we are now BIG over our perceived fears.

We can utilize this method with any type of fear. There are true fears. For example, to believe we are completely safe in this world is to be naive. There are people who inhabit our world that have the ability to hurt and destroy other people. One could choose to live in fear that something might happen to us or a loved one. This true fear could rule one's mind if left unchecked. In extreme cases, one could develop agoraphobia, the fear of the outside world. This disorder causes one to feel safe only within the confines of their own home and can cause some people to withdraw entirely from human contact. What could start out as a true, small fear can develop into an unjustifiably huge true fear that can forever change our lives for the worse.

The other option is to deal with a fear at its inception. In this same example, when a fearful thought of what could happen to us in the world comes to mind, we could take that thought captive and say, "God has sent his angel armies around me to protect me." As we confess with our mouth the protection of God, we begin to change the thought patterns in our brain. In doing this, our brain says, "Oh we are protected and should not fear." A dynamic takes place that stops the signal of fear.

After we confess the positive, there are other actions we can take to combat this fear. Rather than shrinking from the world, we can be proactive. We can, for example, be aware of our surroundings, be able to defend ourselves and be ready with a game plan in place, should the worst of situations occur. Being prepared hand-in-hand with a Godly mindset will keep this type of true fear in check. But we may have to continuously perform these exercises of faith.

The moment a fear is acknowledged in our mind, we should immediately capture it and direct it. The Bible teaches us about this, for example,

> We demolish arguments and **every** pretension that sets itself up against the knowledge of God, and we **take captive every thought** to make it obedient to Christ (2 Corinthians 10:5, emphasis added).

> Do not conform to the pattern of this world, but be transformed by the renewing of your mind. Then you will be able to test and approve what God's will is—His good, pleasing and perfect will (Romans 12:2).

The word of God tells us to take every thought captive and make it obedient to Christ. The moment a bad thought arises, speak to that thought and tell it why it is not true. Next, as scripture teaches us, we must tell ourselves what is true from God's perspective. This reshapes and "transforms" our mind. Beginning with this and setting into action a plan gives us the ability to control our fear and be BIG over it. This takes practice and diligence, and I often find myself performing this over and over on the same fear. As this is practiced, fear truly begins to fade and diminish. Acknowledge, attack, and for heaven's sake, don't feed your fears!

LEANING INTO FEAR

Years ago, while on a vacation in the Caribbean, I decided to take an introduction to scuba adventure course. I had no diving experience whatsoever except for my mad skills in snorkeling. I got on the dive boat that took us where I would learn to dive. I received a ten minute instruction of do's and don'ts. The instructor finished her talk with the statement, "Follow my instructions and you won't find yourself in trouble once in the water. Remember, this is a serious sport and can be life threatening." She handed me my equipment and expected me to "dive" into this sport. I remember thinking, "How will I remember all this information? Will I do it correctly?" Nervous and uncertain about whether I wanted to continue, I got into the water all geared up to descend into the deep. As I began to descend, I found that I couldn't get a complete breath of air from my regulator. I resurfaced and then tried again, with the same results. I remembered talking to myself saying, "Come on, Dawna, don't let this fear get you." But I still was not able to get a full breath from my regulator. I *was* afraid to dive, but I also discovered that I had an unbalanced regulator, which made it difficult to get a full breath of air. I never did descend. Although I was relieved as I got back into the boat, I was also disappointed that I did not complete my goal of diving.

Months later, I received a Christmas present from my husband—a completely paid for scuba diving class! You can imagine my excitement, NOT! I had developed a fear of not being able to breathe associated with diving. I did not want to take the class nor did I have any desire to ever scuba dive again. But my husband pushes and stretches me like no one can. He promised, if I tried it for a second time and I did not like it, I could quit.

Frightened, I decided I would give it a try. I began the classes and had a much better experience. I learned the skills of diving in a pool, which gave me some comfort that if I needed to ascend quickly, I could. One of the tests I had to pass was experiencing what it is like to run out of air. I tossed and turned at night over this test. This was my fear—not being able to breathe under water. The day arrived for this task to be demonstrated. I remember telling myself it would be okay. After all, I was just in a pool, for Pete's sake! Then the time came, while at the bottom of the pool, the instructor turned off my air supply and I slowly began to feel the loss of air. When I no longer could take a breath, I gave him the signal that I was out of air. He quickly opened the life-giving valve, and I resumed breathing. I did it! I passed the one test I was certain I would fail.

Before I became a certified diver, I had to perform all my newly learned skills in an open water dive. This took place in the real elements, where things truly can go wrong. Once this hurdle was achieved, my husband wasted no time—he had booked us a scuba diving trip to Mexico just two days after my open water certification was completed. Did I say he pushes and stretches me like no one can?

Upon our arrival, our first dive consisted of a drift dive (where the current takes you) and a dive in a cenote near Cancun (where in places, you cannot come up for air). Oh, and did I mention that I am a bit claustrophobic? I was nervous about both dives. This time, I leaned into my fear. I faced it head on and conquered it. I completed the dives, elated that I didn't allow fear to overwhelm me. This fear held both truth and lies. There are true dangers in scuba diving. There are also false fears that grew in my head about diving. However, I chose to lean in, press in, and press on. Taking a warrior stance against my fear, I succeeded.

I have been a certified scuba diver now for almost ten years, and the thought of diving still makes me nervous. The difference is that I press on and face the fear. When I do this, I feel like I can take on the world. This is how God created us to live. Free of fear and the ability to tackle fear when it rears its ugly head. The world's greatest UFC fighter, Jon "Bones" Jones says this, "You can fight your fear or give into it." This is now how I approach life, with fight.

WHO ELSE FEARED?

One of my favorite Bible characters is Peter. He was impulsive, loved recklessly, said the wrong things at the wrong times, doubted, and denied Jesus. Yet, he was transformed into an amazing preacher and healer who learned about true faith in Jesus. In Mathew 14:22–33, we see Peter and the disciples in a boat during a terrible storm. Jesus appears to them, walking on the water. Scripture tells us that the disciples were terrified and thought Jesus was a ghost. Jesus tells them to not be afraid and identifies Himself. Peter responds, "Lord, if it is You, tell me to come to You on the water." Jesus calls Peter to come. Peter got out of the boat and walked on the water.

However, Peter had one problem; he allowed the circumstances of his surroundings to overcome him. He took his eyes off Jesus. Once he did, he began to sink, along with his faith. My dear sisters, we can be fearful and still climb out of the boat and walk to Jesus. We can acknowledge our fear before Him. We can call out, "Jesus I am afraid, but I will keep my eyes on you!" And as we climb out of the boat, we walk on the turbulent waves of life towards the only One who can calm the storms in our lives. As we refuse to look at the conditions of our storms and keep our eyes fixed on Jesus, we are feeding our faith and starving our fears. This brings us closer to Him. When we get out of the boat, we lean into our fear and head into the arms of the fearless One.

What steps of faith do we need to begin to address our fears and break down our walls of resentment? First, we should take them to Jesus and begin the process of growing faith and starving fears. Then we can lean into our fears and start new lives of transformation—without walls of fear and resentment.

So, is the peace of Jesus ruling in your heart? We are all capable of living with peace in our hearts. In 2 Peter 1:3, Peter says, *"His divine power has given us **everything** we need for a godly life through our knowledge of Him who called us by His own glory and goodness"* (emphasis added). Jesus has given us everything we need in this given moment. Let us look to Him and release our fears and resentments into His life-giving hands. What is it that you need to let go of at this moment, so that you do not live in fear and resentment?

Fear of Momith stealing the kids!
Being a slave of fear!

KITES AND SNAKES

One day, I was walking my two Huskies. As we approached a neighbor's house, the three of us spotted someone trying to fly a kite. My Husky, Hanah, caught sight of this and was terrified. She turned around and headed back in the direction of home, until the leash stopped her in her tracks. I kept telling her it was okay, and attempted to move forward. She was terrified and not paying attention to me. She continued to pull the opposite way towards home. She wanted nothing to do with approaching that flying thing in the air. I laughed, because my stubborn, frightened Husky shortened our walk because of her fear of this unidentified object.

The following day, we walked the same route and came upon another, I thought, *unidentified object*. Something was moving in the grass, presumably a rodent. As both Huskies pulled forward, ready to pounce, I saw that it was a large snake. I hate snakes! I swiftly pulled them away from the danger, and we continued on our way. As we headed for home, I was sure to keep them on the opposite side of the street to avoid the slithering beast. It puzzled me that my Husky could be afraid of something she shouldn't be fearful of and not be fearful of the thing she should. But then I thought, *Isn't that like us?* Sometimes we fear things that will cause us no harm (false fears), or we can have no fear when we really should.

What are the 'kites' in your life? The things that you fear and shouldn't? What are the 'snakes' in your life that you're not afraid of when you should be? Some of my *kites* are fear of failure. However, I am going to fail from time to time. That is just a known fact. I am afraid of losing control, but I truly don't have control. On the other hand, on a daily basis, I am not as mindful or as afraid of spiritual things, that could harm me like temptation, or pride. These things can bite me if I'm not careful. I should be more cognizant of them in my daily walk. We all have *kites* and *snakes*. We must grasp a correct perspective on our fears if we want to see our walls come crumbling down.

JERICHO GIRLS' RESPONSE: CAN YOU IDENTIFY WITH THEM?

- *It is difficult for me to expose my fears and resentment. It is tough to examine yourself that way.*

- *I do not share stuff like this with most—only with the few who are in my inner circle.*

- *I am so happy to learn that God examines our hearts with a flash-light of love.*

JERICHO GIRLS' TOOL BOX:

Sledgehammer those walls!

 "Be strong and courageous. Do not be afraid; do not be discouraged, for the Lord your God will be with you wherever you go" (Joshua 1:9).

TRAINING YOUR SOUL AND BREAKING DOWN WALLS:

Spend some time in prayer humbly asking God for the grace to see clearly what walls of fear, and/or resentment you might have. You might want to journal your feelings. When you discuss your resentments and fears before God, what emotions come to the surface? Bring these feelings to God and sit with them quietly before Him. Write down how He might have you deal with them.

Fear	Resentment	emotions come to surface	How to deal
H stealing the kids		panic, saddness, disappointment	prayer, psalm 37, Jeremiah 29:12 I will listen to you—

11

HEALTHY WALLS

MY WORST ENEMY

When I think of my worst enemy, my mind swirls with people like terrorists and murderers. The other thing that comes to mind is the fallen angel, Satan. Not the image of red tights, horns, and pitchfork, but the beautiful fallen angel, miserable, evil, and roaming the earth to see whom he can destroy. He is a reality and my worst enemy—or is he?

The more time I spend with women, the more I realize that our biggest enemy is ourselves. We women are so hard on ourselves. We spend so much time beating ourselves up—WAY too much time! We tend to focus on our shortcomings rather than our gifts. We can beat ourselves up for just about anything: a wrong word said, a divorce that we didn't want to happen, growing up in a dysfunctional family and unsuccessful at breaking the mold, not beautiful enough, not smart enough, too introverted, too extroverted, mistakes in the past that we can't let go of. . . . Name it, and we beat ourselves up about it.

We are able to see the beauty, and not the faults, of our girlfriends, but can't love ourselves enough to see our same goodness within. In order to conquer this enemy, we need to build a healthy wall of forgiveness. Forgiving ourselves is one of the healthiest things we can do.

I listened to one of my friends give advice to another friend, someone who is very hard on herself. My ministering friend had such words of wisdom. She posed the questions: "Do you think that God makes mistakes? Do you think that God made a mistake when He put you into that family?" She continued, "The God I know doesn't make mistakes, so let me ask you this." Then she simply said, "What will you do with the gift of being born into a dysfunctional family?" What a powerful, insightful question. What she is saying is, I can have situations in my life that are beyond difficult; but what I do with that 'gift' and how I apply it to my life make all the difference in the world of my heart. She is saying, "Stop! Break the mold; quit living in the shadow of your situation, and certainly quit beating yourself up about it." Yes, we need to address the need for change in our lives; but we have to begin the change by *moving forward*, not by living with regrets and tearing ourselves down. We can quit being so hard on ourselves, forgive ourselves and move on.

If I can love and forgive myself, then I can have a healthy wall that blocks self-destruction and only allows healthy self-forgiveness. I can give myself the gift of giving myself a break. This healthy wall is intended to be in place. When it is in place and I fail in my life and I make mistakes, I take them to God and acknowledge them before Him. When I do this, do you know what happens? He forgives me. Yes, that is right. He forgives me and never brings up the situation again. If that is God's response to us, then shouldn't it be our response to ourselves too? Forgive yourself, sister. If you don't, you are placing yourself in a dangerous position—one that denies God's capability to forgive and one that creates an unhealthy wall around your heart. This wall keeps God out, and virtually boxes God in. *This wall* needs to come down. *Healthy walls* are walls that keep God close to your heart. Once you get a taste of God's reconciliation, that is all you will want.

The women in my life are so amazing. I drink from their fountain of knowledge. As I reflect on the conversation with my two friends, I realize that we are our own worst enemy. We fail to recognize that we have the ability to transform our failures into 'gifts'. When we simply make the decision to not beat ourselves up and instead view life experiences and difficult situations as gifts, we utilize everything that is handed to us for good and to better us. But we continually beat ourselves up over everything, from the simplest things to the most serious issues in our lives. Why do we do this? Why are we so hard on ourselves? Today is the day that we can build a wall that will forever change our lives for good. The wall of self-forgiveness is for everyone. Shouldn't you have this healthy wall too?

What does this look like? Understanding that God has forgiven us should evoke a response of self-forgiveness. Since God forgives us, then our response should be to forgive ourselves. I believe it is easier to live in the space where you are forgiven by God than it is to live in self-forgiveness. However, as God's warriors, we are called to be a new self, putting on Christ, forgiving and loving ourselves, and seeing ourselves through God's eyes. When we can do this, we are able to build healthy walls around our hearts—the kind of walls a warrior should have.

AND STILL MY OWN WORST ENEMY

Once we begin to build our healthy walls of self-forgiveness, we need to examine another behavior that keeps us from maintaining healthy walls. It's something we do subconsciously—*comparison.* This sneaky little act tries to tell us where we are doing well and where we are not. What typically results from comparison is seeing others as being better than we are. This inevitably tends to make us believe that we are failures.

Comparison can also lead to seeing ourselves as better than others, which can create unhealthy pride in our hearts. However, women tend to compare themselves as 'less than'. This leads to our feelings of inadequacy. We then tend to see others as having more: more talent, more beauty, more intelligence, more liked, more spiritual, or more blessed than we are. Ultimately, we find ourselves wishing for what we don't have. Comparing is not what we should be doing. This is

117

like the "provoking and envying" that the Apostle Paul admonishes against in Galatians 5:26. Paul continues in Galatians 6:3–4, "If anyone thinks they are something when they are not, they deceive themselves. Each one should test their own actions. Then they can take pride in themselves alone without comparing themselves to someone else." Already (see Galatians 6:1–2) he has advised restoring gently one caught in a sin, and then tells them to "Watch yourselves or you also may be tempted." He tells them to carry each other's burdens. Paul returns to the need for self-evaluation. He instructs them to carefully examine their own work, and not on the basis of someone else's. He is telling them and us, do not compare yourself to others.

I still find myself comparing from time to time. The difference now is that I recognize it quicker and I am able to stop myself when I begin. I had a conversation with a friend who told me, "You do so much. You are always there for your friends, your family, and, on top of that, you work and do ministry. How do you do it all? I need to be more like you." *Funny,* I thought. So I shared with her that I had just left a mentoring session and I had told my mentor the same thing about her; that she does so much and that I would like to be more like her. My friend was comparing herself to me and I was comparing myself to my mentor.

Let's take our eyes off someone else and refocus them on ourselves and the wondrous inner gifts, strengths, and beauty that we have been gifted with. Let's be grateful for what we have. If we begin doing this, then we start a paradigm shift that focuses on the goodness of God and what He has blessed us with.

We need to be able to look at someone else without comparing ourselves to them. We can then share in the joys of their God-given gifts, knowing that their gifts are unique to them and ours are unique to us. We can then appreciate each other and not compare. We need to live in that healthy confine and surround our hearts with it.

Remember, you were created for a purpose; you have a unique and divine calling on your life. This will point you to live with an eternal perspective and free you from comparing yourself to others. Let it remind you whose you are and how unique and special you truly are.

A Woman and a Scarlet Cord

A young Canaanite woman lived in Jericho, the wicked city that was under God's judgment. This city was known for its worship of idols and false gods. This woman made her living as a prostitute, her name was Rahab. We don't know what brought her to this way of life, but we know that this pagan culture probably taught her that this was normal or acceptable. I can sense the stirrings in Rahab's heart that made her long for more.

She heard the stories spread throughout Jericho, that the God of Israel was with His people. She heard how God brought the Israelites out of Egypt, how He parted the Red Sea, about the Israelites wandering in the wilderness, manna from heaven, water coming out of a rock, and, the Israelites conquering the Amorites. I can visualize Rahab going about her daily work and wondering about the Israelite's stories of protection and redemption. Where was this one true God who redeemed so many? Her heart longed for the One who _could_ change the course of her life, who was able to quench a worn out, parched, and thirsty soul.

She identified her deepest desire to be known and to be loved by the one true God. But how could she obtain it? Why would He be interested in someone like her? I can imagine her sense of unworthiness. I can hear her talking to herself, beating herself up for the life that she either chose or that was chosen for her. I can taste her bitterness, and visualize her comparing herself to other women that lived behind the walls of Jericho. She longed for hope. That day arrived when two Israelite spies entered her home, turning her world upside down. That day she realized that she had the chance of hope for a lifetime.

She had decisions to make; do I hide behind my walls of fear and resentment? Do I demean myself and compare myself to other women who might be better fit for the job of hiding Israelite spies? Or do I break out, forgive myself, and live beyond the walls that I have known for so many years. She had only seconds to decide what she would do in the moment these Israelite spies came bursting into her life and into her home.

She decided to break free. She jumped into the arms of risky faith and radical trust and into the arms of a God that she had known through stories. She was about to experience Him in a new way. Rahab chose to hide the spies on her roof. The King of Jericho sent a message to Rahab asking her to bring out the men that came to her house, informing her that they were spies. By the time she got the message, it is too late. Rahab had already made a heart decision to move forward and not look back. She wanted to know the God of the Israelites. If it meant hiding spies, then that was what she was going to do.

The king's men came crashing through her door, questioning and inquiring about the spies. Rahab shook, her heart racing. *What have I done?* She quickly came up with a story that the spies had been there, but she did not know where they had come from or who they were. She continued to tell them with a reluctant voice that when the city gates were about to be closed for the day, they escaped from the city. The king's men believed her and left. She pressed her back against the door of her home, as tears streamed down her face. Her body quivered at the thought of lying to the king of Jericho, considering all of what might happen to her if he found out.

What to do now? There was no turning back. Did she make a mistake, risking her life on stories of a God that could save, rescue, and forever change her life? It didn't matter. In Rahab's heart, she was determined to find truth. This was her one chance to see for herself if the God of the Israelites was a true and living God. She went to the roof to confess to the spies her belief in their God. Joshua 2: 8–11 records her confession:

> Before the spies lay down for the night, she went up on the roof and said to them, "I know that the LORD has given you this land and that a great fear of you has fallen on us, so that all who live in this country are melting in fear because of you. We have heard how the LORD dried up the water of the Red Sea for you when you came out of Egypt, and what you did to Sihon and Og, the two kings of the Amorites east of the Jordan, whom you completely destroyed. When we heard of it, our hearts melted in fear and everyone's courage failed because of you, for the LORD your God is God in heaven above and on the earth below."

Rahab's heart melted with fear of what the one true God could do. She acknowledged before the spies that she believed in the power of their God. She asked them to swear an oath to her, vowing protection for her and her family. The spies agreed, if Rahab agreed not to tell anyone of their visit. They told her to gather her family and keep them at her home, as the Israelites were coming to destroy Jericho (Joshua 2: 21).

> So she let them down by a rope through the window, for the house she lived in was part of the city wall. She said to them, "Go to the hills so the pursuers will not find you. Hide yourselves there three days until they return, and then go on your way."
>
> Now the men had said to her, "This oath you made us swear will not be binding on us unless, when we enter the land, you have tied this scarlet cord in the window through which you let us down, and unless you have brought your father and mother, your brothers and all your family into your house. If any of them go outside your house into the street, their blood will be on their own heads; we will not be responsible. As for those who are in the house with you, their blood will be on our head if a hand is laid on them. But if you tell what we are doing, we will be released from the oath you made us swear."
>
> "Agreed," she replied. "Let it be as you say."
>
> So she sent them away, and they departed. And she tied the scarlet cord in the window.

The God of Israel was coming for her. He was going to protect her. However, God required action from Rahab. She willingly obeyed and she did as instructed. She tied the scarlet cord in her window.

All of Rahab's hopes were tied to one scarlet cord hanging from her window. She was vulnerable. She had let down her wall and let the men of Israel and their God into her heart. Would they betray her? Would they destroy her and her family, or keep their promise? This is something she would never know unless she was able to bring down her wall, share her heart, and lean into her fear—which she so bravely did. That night, she was real with the men, as she shared her heart's desires, longing for a God who could rescue her. How her heart was melted with the fear of Him and the Israelites. She must have wrestled with her decision to be true to her heart, or to take the safe path and hide behind her wall of familiarity.

goal

121

The time between the spies leaving her house and returning to take Jericho must have seemed like an eternity to Rahab. Then the day came when the Israelites conquered Jericho. When they saw the scarlet cord hanging from Rahab's window, she was rescued. The story doesn't end there. God used the rescued heroine, Rahab in a mighty way. Yes, our God uses the least likely, the sinner, the liar, and the brokenhearted who hides behind her heart's walls.

When Rahab dared to open her heart to bring down the walls that kept her prisoner, God did something huge. He rescued her. Not only did He save Rahab, He placed her in the lineage of Jesus. Imagine all the ways God could use you, if you would just open your heart, bring down the walls of your heart and throw Him 'a rope'.

OWN WHOSE YOU ARE

The only way we can begin to erect healthy walls of forgiveness and not compare ourselves to others is to understand whose child we are. Despite our disobedience, God still sent His son for us. God thought that you were worth it—period. I don't understand it. I cannot fathom such a pure and holy love, but just because it is difficult to comprehend doesn't mean we shouldn't accept it. We can take this free gift of love and simply own it. Yes, we make mistakes daily, but we need to take them to Him who understands. Then simply let go and allow His all-encompassing love to envelop us. "Let us then approach God's throne of grace with confidence, so that we may receive mercy and find grace to help us in our time of need" (Hebrews 4:16). When we are wrapped up in God's pure love, we can know whose we are—we belong to Him. Then we can own who we are.

Michael Card says in his book, *A Fragile Stone*, that God uses the puzzle pieces of our lives. "There comes a moment in our lives when some of the pieces of the puzzle come together—where all our past experiences, both good and bad, are brought to bear in causing us to become who God intends us to be." We need to understand that despite our mess-ups, God puts the puzzle pieces together. He uses our mistakes, combining them with our goodness to create a beautiful puzzle picture.

Have you ever put together a puzzle? The person putting the puzzle together knows what the puzzle picture is going to look like when it is complete. Do you remember having a few of those odd shaped puzzle pieces that did not fit anywhere on the puzzle when you were putting it together? I would always put those odd pieces off to the side to see where I could use them as the puzzle came together as it got further along. Those are representative of the *bad* pieces or the mistakes in our lives.

God does that too. He says, "Let's put that over here and I will use it for my glory as I see fit." As He places the pieces into the pattern of our puzzled lives, we begin to see the beautiful picture that He has created us to be. When we own whose we are and live free from dwelling on our mistakes, we then can see God piecing together each part of our lives. He uses the good along with the bad to make beautiful scenes in the puzzle of our lives.

Do you believe God is piecing the puzzle of your life together, using each piece and crafting a gorgeous scene called your story? He is immensely creative placing each puzzle piece into place, using each one carefully and skillfully. When we live knowing Whose we are and Who is placing our pieces, then we are free to live with healthy walls and great freedom.

Sara Young, *Jesus calling* May 9;

> *Don't be so hard on yourself. I can bring good even out of your mistakes. Your finite mind tends to look backward, longing to undo decisions you have come to regret. This is a waste of time and energy, leading only to frustration. Instead of floundering in the past, release your mistakes to Me. Look to Me in trust, anticipating that My infinite creativity can weave both good choices and bad into a lovely design.*

When we construct healthy walls of forgiveness, promise, esteem, and walls of love around our hearts, we begin to live with the walls that every warrior should have. Then we are living out our God-given design, as warriors who fight to bring down walls that don't belong, and replacing them with healthy walls. Own it and fight for it.

JERICHO GIRLS' RESPONSE: CAN YOU IDENTIFY WITH THEM?

- *It is difficult to forgive others— let alone myself.*

- *I compare myself to others because I am always worried about what someone else thinks of me. I am constantly sizing myself up to another.*

- *Wow! Understanding Whose I am frees me to live without all this mess in my life.*

JERICHO GIRLS' TOOL BOX:

Quit trying to *measure* up to others.

"If anyone thinks they are something when they are not, they deceive themselves. Each one should test their own actions. Then they can take pride in themselves alone, without comparing themselves to someone else, for each one should carry their own load" (Galatians 6:3–5).

TRAINING YOUR SOUL AND BREAKING DOWN WALLS:

Spend a day focused on your inner beauty and not your external. Think about the gifts that God has given you. Can you go a whole day in public without wearing makeup? Can you wear something frumpy and still feel beautiful? What do you need to give up, to remind yourself how beautiful you are without those "things"? Decide what that is, and then spend a whole day going without that thing and meditating on the beautiful you—without comparing yourself to others.

12

READY FOR BATTLE

THE BATTLE IN MY CLOSET

Every day I go to my closet and decide which outfit best suits my schedule. If I have a meeting, I might pick out a suit; if I am speaking, I might wear a dress; if I am showing property, I might be inclined to wear a business outfit with comfortable shoes. Lunch with friends means jeans and a shirt. Every day I am forced to decide what I should wear to coordinate with my day's agenda.

This is an essential ritual done day-in and day-out. Each day I struggle with what to wear. As I spend my mornings in battle with my wardrobe, there is another battle raging in me that I am unconscious of—the spiritual battle raging in the heavenly realms. The battle in my closet should begin with thinking about my spiritual suit rather than trying to figure out what earthly clothes to put on. My daily dressing routine should consist of first putting on my spiritual outfit.

Ephesians 6:10–12 tells us that we should dress in the full armor of God each day so that we can take a stand. In essence, it tells us that we are to do this because our battle is of a spiritual nature. There is a battle being fought every second, therefore, we need to dress for it.

> *Finally, be strong in the Lord and in His mighty power. Put on the full armor of God, so that you can take your stand against the devil's schemes. For our struggle is not against flesh and blood, but against the rulers, against the authorities, against the powers of this dark world and against the spiritual forces of evil in the heavenly realms* (Ephesians 6:10–12).

It's easy to forget that there is more going on than what we see. This passage clearly states that we fight with "powers of this dark world and against spiritual forces of evil in the heavenly realms." Because I tend to get so wrapped up in the world of 'me', it's easy to go through my days without acknowledging this spiritual battle taking place around me. My day focuses on *my* daily schedule, *my* prayers, what *I* am going to eat, what *I* am going to do, what *I* will wear. . . .

All these thoughts consume my mind more than what is truly important—"How will I dress my soul today? How will I protect my mind? How will I shield my heart in a healthy way?" These are the questions that should occupy my closet time. Not with my eyes searching for the right outfit, but on my knees, visualizing my necessary spiritual wardrobe, dressing each day in the essentials.

> *Therefore put on the full armor of God, so that when the day of evil comes, you may be able to stand your ground, and after you have done everything, to stand. Stand firm then, with the belt of truth buckled around your waist, with the breastplate of righteousness in place, and with your feet fitted with the readiness that comes from the gospel of peace. In addition to all this, take up the shield of faith, with which you can extinguish all the flaming arrows of the evil one. Take the helmet of salvation and the sword of the Spirit, which is the word of God. And pray in the Spirit on all occasions with all kinds of prayers and requests. With this in mind, be alert and always keep on praying for all the Lord's people* (Ephesians 6:13–18).

Each day is new, and there are choices to be made. Each day, we will encounter spiritual battles in the spiritual realm, battles within ourselves, and battles with others. We need to prepare for these. Buckle the belt of truth around our waist; start the morning with God's word—reading our Bible, being in prayer, and spending time with Him in His truth. If we cannot distinguish God's truth, then it is difficult to forge forward into the day's battles.

Put on the breastplate of righteousness. We need to guard our hearts, surround it with truth and safeguard it from inner attacks from ourselves, the enemy, and from others. The heart is a vital organ. We need to keep it protected, not by building walls that keep us isolated and hidden, but by putting on the breast plate of true protection. We must build healthy walls so that we are ready to defeat anything that compromises our heart and our desire to please God. Protecting it, is of the utmost importance.

doing what is right in God's eyes.

Place on your feet the readiness of the gospel of peace. There are many paths with twists, turns, and obstacles. Our feet need to be equipped to take us in the right direction. We need to be warriors. As women, we don't always see ourselves as warriors, but we are.

Think about what we, as women, accomplish in a day. We do it all, so we are certainly equipped to fight battles for God. In fact, do you know that God has titled "women" using a word related to the military? In Genesis 2:18, God says it is not good that man should be alone so He created a "helper." The word used in Hebrew is *ezer* which means to aid—help, protect, and defend. If we look at the context of every other use of the word ezer in the scripture, you will see that ezer refers to either God or military allies. In all other cases, the one giving the help is superior to the one receiving the help. Did you know that you were created to be a warrior to protect and defend? Equip your feet for battle and follow the right path, knowing that each day along your path, you will be walking through a mine field. Don't dread them, but be ready for them.

The shield of faith is necessary to protect yourself. Scripture tells us it is impossible to please God without faith. Therefore, have the faith that enables you to conquer the day and the confines of your heart.

We must put on the helmet of salvation. Many battles begin in the mind. Our thoughts need to be protected. "Watch your thoughts; they become words. Watch your words; they become actions. Watch your actions; they become habits. Watch your habits; they become character. Watch your character; it becomes your destiny." Lao Tzu.

What begins in the mind can lead to choices that direct our paths. That's why Scripture tells us to wear a helmet of salvation. Protecting

127

our thoughts is of utmost importance. When we protect our minds, we are better equipped to keep our focus on an eternal perspective. When we keep a rule on our minds, we are able to see things more clearly. This keeps our walls in check, too. When we keep our minds free from thoughts that keep us captive—thoughts of fear, resentment, comparison, rejection, and whatever else we can conjure up, then we are free to keep an eternal perspective and focus on thoughts that matter. We are then able to think about God and love, patience, kindness, goodness, self-control, and humility. These thoughts allow us to keep our healthy walls up and stop our unhealthy walls from being built.

Finally, the sword of the spirit. The Word of God is needed to complete our wardrobe. Verbalizing Scripture aloud throughout the day speaks things into being. Just as God spoke things into being during creation, so we need to speak things into our lives. The power of words is exactly that—powerful! I am not promoting speaking things that *we want* into existence. Because we were created in God's image, He gives us the ability to speak with power and authority just like He did when He brought forth the earth, sun, moon, and stars. We have God's power within us. When we speak as He does, our battles are already won *according to His will*.

I practice this when my husband road races. When I feel fear creeping into my heart and become anxious before his race begins, I speak God's word out loud. I will quote scriptures such as, "For God did not give us a spirit of timidity [or fear], but a spirit of power, of love and of self-discipline" (2 Timothy 1:7), or, "all the days ordained for me [and David] were written in your book before one of them came to be" (Psalm 139:16).

Speaking God's word and verbalizing it does something in the heavenly realms of our hearts that stops fear, that stops anxiety or whatever emotion we are dealing with. The sword of the Spirit is powerful and leads us safely into battle. Each day presents before us a new battle. As God's warriors, we are called to be dressed and ready. Now go put on your armor and get dressed for the day.

VICTORIOUS BUT NOT ON OUR OWN

After I dress myself physically, and spiritually, each day I march into battle and something happens. I charge forward into the day attempting to take it on by myself. But battles are not won on our own. Do we ever see a soldier going into battle alone? No. They are part of a combat unit with other soldiers who train and fight together. One of the most important things you can do when you face each day is to have an alliance with other women who love you and will fight with you.

The women in my life give me advice, call me out, push me to do better than I think I can do myself, and we all do this in community. If you are attempting to do things on your own, the most important thing you can do for yourself is to get connected with others. This can begin in a small group or with a one-on-one friend. Community is where my journey began. When I was invited to a summer Bible study, I went very reluctantly. When I attended the first study, I thought it would be a six-week journey and that would be it. But these women stole my heart and ten years later I cannot imagine doing life without them.

As women, we tend to have a hard time asking for help. Many of us believe that if we ask for help, it means we are weak. However, I believe the opposite is true. When we ask for help, it aids in building alliances that strengthens our combat forces so that we can go into battle fully prepared. If we remove the false belief that doing things on our own makes us strong, allying with the right people to help us (and help them) along the path of life, then we are truly strong.

We also need help from the top. We need help from the Commander-in-Chief—God. We need to receive our daily orders, and then march into battle. Our daily orders come in the form of prayer. So before we just march into battle, we need to remember the tremendous importance of prayer!

When we look at the story of Joshua and the instructions given to him by God on how the walls of Jericho would come down, it was through prayer and God's instruction. In Joshua 5, shortly before they were to march around the walls of Jericho, God asks Joshua to have the men circumcised. This seems like an odd request from God. The men needed to be strong for battle, but instead God puts them out of commission just prior to going into battle. What does this tells us as God's warriors? It tells us that it is God who fights our battles—not us alone or by our own physical strength.

The story of Joshua reminds us that we are weak without God and we can't win battles without Him. We need God. We will never be successful on our own until we relinquish control and quit attempting to do things alone. We need God, and we need others. The story of Joshua teaches us that each day we are to circumcise our hearts (spiritually speaking). Each day we have a choice to make: *Will I do it my way or God's way?* When we choose our way things get messy. When we choose His perfect way, things go much better.

Our walls can only come down by prayer, with God's help, and the support of our warrior sisters. Not by shear force or by ourselves. When we align with God and our warrior sisters in Christ, we bring down walls through prayer and the enemy is melting with fear. When Jesus cast out demons, they feared Him. "What do you want with us Son of God?" These demons were melting with fear in the presence of Jesus. When Jesus was tempted in the desert, He resisted Satan through the word, prayer, and fasting. When Jesus raised the dead, prayer came first. The power of prayer is essential to equip ourselves for battle. Step aside from a false sense of ability to do it alone and let God step in and lead the battle.

EQUIPPED

When we fight like a Warrior for God and by God's ways, we fight with vision, determination, and compassion. We need to have God's vision before we can see the victory. The walls around our hearts need to be seen through the "General's" perspective. We should ask ourselves, "How would God see me deal with this? How would God have me bring down this wall?" God always wants us to submit to His will. We need to give up our rights and the hunt for our self-interest and stand fast to what God would have us do. This is how we go equipped into battle.

Once we have the correct vision, we need to charge into battle determined. We need to fix our eyes on the purpose of the battle and pledge to a resolution. When we build walls, we are giving up, and that's not what God's warriors do. Warriors do not hide behind walls, rather they charge in, and bring down the things that hinder and threaten. Walls hinder, and threaten us, because they isolate and prevent real relationships.

We also need to fight with a compassionate heart. We shouldn't fight by retaliation, through hurt, resentment, fear, façades, or the use of words in a way to destroy someone. Fight in a way that honors God. When we put on the armor of God, we are putting on Christ.

How did Christ react? He reacted with love and compassion, telling the truth in love. When we are hurt or afraid of getting hurt by others, it is necessary not to build walls, but rather fight to keep our walls down and our hearts shielded with Christ.

How did David fight Goliath? David told King Saul that he would fight the giant Goliath. When King Saul saw that David was serious, he dressed David in armor. But it was too big, heavy, and cumbersome for him and so he discarded it. This gives us insight into what we shouldn't rely on and Whom we *should* rely on. Saul thought that David would be protected by layers of armor. David had a different heart. He knew that he had relied on God to protect him while tending sheep all those years. God had protected him and his flock from lions and bears. David had no armor then. He continued to believe the same God who kept him safe from the wild beasts, would protect him from the giant Philistine. In David's mind, God protected him from everything. There was no difference between this giant and the lions and bears he had faced in the past.

As David approached the giant Philistine, the Philistine mocked him and shouted out insults. David said to the Philistine, "You come against me with sword and spear and javelin, but I come against you in the name of the LORD Almighty, the God of the armies of Israel, whom you have defied. This day the LORD will deliver you into my hands, and I'll strike you down and cut off your head. This very day I will give the carcasses of the Philistine army to the birds and the wild animals, and the whole world will know that there is a God in Israel.

All those gathered here will know that it is not by sword, or spear that the LORD saves; for the battle is the LORD's, and He will give all of you into our hands. As the Philistine moved closer to attack him, David ran quickly toward the battle line to meet him" (I Samuel 17:45–48).

David fought and won the battle through the protection of God. Not through hiding behind armor, or a false sense of protection. He did not use hurtful words like the Philistine. Rather, David simply delineated the expected outcome, which may have seemed a little harsh to the sensitive Philistines. All he did was believe that the battle was God's and charged into battle. He had the correct vision. He charged forward in faith, trusting in God, and fought a good, clean, fight using only the words of the Lord.

And what happened? David defeated Goliath with one stone. We too can fight against the walls of our hearts, equipped with the word of God. We can allow God to fight for us when our hearts are threatened. You are equipped so don't retreat from the giants in your life. Rather, face them and bring down those walls! "No, in all these things we are more than conquerors through Him who loved us" (Romans 8:37).

KNOWING IS DIFFERENT THAN DOING

I sent a friend my manuscript on the chapter I wrote about her—the one who was struggling with walls of resentment towards her husband. I asked her if there were any changes about her story I needed to make or if there was anything too intrusive to share. I waited with no response. All sorts of thoughts raced through my mind, "Did I offend her? Did she not like it? Why was she being so silent? Something must be wrong." One day passed with no response. I finally decided I needed to put on the helmet of salvation and get the correct thinking going. I began to pray that my friend would receive what God would have her hear while reading the manuscript. I prayed for myself too, that I would receive her criticism with grace and that God would take control of my anxious thoughts. After all, we have been friends for many years; surely she knows my love for her and that I would never say anything to hurt her.

Day two came and went. So did day three. On the fourth day, I received a call from her. She said, "I read your manuscript." Then silence. She finally spoke and said, "Sister! I have to tell you what happened this weekend. I read the story you wrote about me. As I read it, a flood of tears welled up and I began to cry." I wasn't sure what to say, so I just waited for her to continue.

"I began to see what I needed to do. You see, I have known this, but knowing it and doing it are two different things. As I read my own story, seeing it before me like that, made it so real. I was crying, and as I finished reading it, my husband walked in. He asked me what was wrong and I told him nothing. I didn't want to talk to him about it. Then a flood of emotions came hurling out. As he stood there I said, I don't want to talk to you, in fact, I don't even like you."

"I couldn't believe what I had just said! Suddenly, it was all out there, and I could not stop the words from coming. Years of non-communication and there it was, laid out before us. He stood there, not knowing what to say." Then he said, "Why don't you like me? We are supposed to be best friends."

"I continued to tell him, you have hurt me many times. When I ask for help, you immediately say hurtful things and I don't want to be hurt anymore. You don't have a clue about my health and couldn't possibly understand my daily pain."

Then he responded, "You have not shared with me for many years. You have not let me in and you always call on someone else when you need help. I am not able to fulfill my role as your husband when you shut me out and don't let me step up."

"Before I knew it, we were in a long, in-depth in conversation, immersed with tears for both of us. It was incredible." I listened with no words except to say, "That is huge, my friend." She told me this was a start in healing their relationship and she committed to work on it.

Do you realize that this is often all we need, just a bit of truth and conversation to get the ball rolling in our relationships? We need to jump into the unknown and do something about our situations.

Making the first crack in our walls is the most important step. Once we do, it starts a chain reaction of change.

I visualize a structure made out of dominos. The first one is knocked over, then the next one falls, and a beautiful display of synchronized, falling dominos takes place. The same is true with the walls of our hearts. If we can just get the first stone knocked over, then the "dominos effect" begins.

Knowing and doing are two different things. You have a choice to make every day. You can choose to shut down and put up walls, or you can be a warrior and work to conquer them.

I watched an interview called, "The Story Behind the Song". It is an interview with Bart Millard, from the band, Mercy Me. He shared the meaning behind his song, *You are I Am*. He said, "There is something within us that should blow our minds, the Spirit living in us. We are not what we used to be. The power of the Spirit lives in us."

We need to remember this every day. We are not who we used to be! The Spirit of God lives in us, and He has the ability to do all things through us. If we have a huge wall before us, He can bring it down. With His help, we can do all things. Philippians 4:13, "I can do everything through Him who gives me strength."

Bart continues, "It's not about bad people trying to be good. It's about redeemed people who still mess up, but can never be removed from the hand of God." Removing walls from our hearts is just like Bart's message. We are redeemed women who are going to mess up and build walls. But when we do, God's love and mercy will help us break them down, and He will never remove His hand from us.

EQUIPPING OTHERS

On our Journey to Jericho, it is important to help others equip themselves as warriors. By helping others with their walls, it helps us to bring down our walls. In Max Lucado's book, *The Cure for the Common Life,* Max states, "For sixteen years, the temple of God had lain in ruins. They had abandoned the work. The reason? Opposition from enemies and indifference from neighbors. But most of all, the job dwarfed them. To build the first temple, Solomon needed seventy thousand carriers, eighty thousand stonecutters, thirty-three hundred foremen and seven years. A gargantuan task! The workers must have thought, 'What difference will my work make?' God's answer: 'Do not despise these small beginnings, for the Lord rejoices to see the work begin' (Zech. 4:10, NLT). Begin—just begin!"

Bringing down the walls of our hearts can seem like the building of the Holy temple. Where does one begin? We might feel like we need eighty thousand stonecutters, and many years to complete the task. Then when we add in the task of helping others with their walls, we now need the thirty-three hundred foremen, and seventy thousand carriers. What I have learned is that as we help others with their heart walls, we relate. We see that we are not alone and typically we share the same experiences and have very similar walls. Helping turns to sharing, and sharing to healing. Therefore, we need to start small, not only with ourselves but with helping others as well. Beginning is the toughest part.

Ever the Battle

After one year with the Jericho Girls, we discovered many things about each other. We learned that we all have walls around our hearts that we are constantly building up and tearing down. We discussed only some of the walls that surround our hearts. We realized that even after one year of sharing, there are many other walls we put in place to hide and protect our hearts.

When I first founded *The Walls of Jericho*, I sent an email to a friend inviting her to join us. She responded that all her walls had come down and she didn't need to meet with us. What I have learned over this last year is that breaking down our walls is something that is never totally finished. It is done over and over again, spanning our lifetimes.

Day-in and day-out we are faced with situations and encounter people who can either cause us to build walls, or bring them down. Ever ongoing, and ever the battle we need to fight. But God has hand crafted us to be warriors, ones who always "fight the good fight," and we are well equipped for battle.

I also realized that I had walls, walls that I was unaware of. I thought I was a transparent person, but the reality was that I had walls: walls of fear, resentment, walls with God, and walls of masks.

I was able to work on deconstructing the walls that were not good for my heart. Identifying my walls was the most difficult. Once I was able to identify them, I was able to move forward in verbalizing, sharing, and dealing with my walls.

One of my greatest challenges is keeping my wall down before God. I struggle with control issues and running on my own strength. God created me to lead, and that is not a bad thing. However, when I attempt to lead without Him is when it becomes an issue. I continually have to remind myself that He has the ultimate plan for my life. I have to decide daily if I am in charge or is God? With God's grace *we* will keep my walls disassembled.

Bringing down that wall of self-sufficiency, and allowing God to be my strength, to take control of my life, even when things seem to go haywire, is my biggest challenge right now. I will continue to work on this with Him.

The most wondrous discovery in our journey to Jericho was the realization of the foundation of our walls— that which underlies our walls. Any wall that we might dream of constructing is typically based on some type of fear. If we can identify what we are afraid of, we will be able to recognize that fear when we encounter it. Then we can identify our wall-building activity. Then and only then, can we bring walls down.

Now that we know that fear drives our wall construction, we need to remember what not to fear; God tells us specifically to "fear not." We can only do this if we give God our fears. He is perfect Love, and only His love can cast out our fears. God is Trustworthy. There should be no walls between us and God. That is where we begin. Once the walls are down before our perfect God, then and only then can we begin to understand healthy walls, boundaries, and how to live within the healthy confines of our hearts, with all fear-based walls constantly coming down. "There is no fear in Love. But perfect Love drives out fear, because fear has to do with punishment. The one who fears is not made perfect in Love" (1 John 4:18).

God is perfect Love, and we can trust Him to help us through anything in this life. He will never fail us or leave us. As we journey with Jesus, breaking down walls and putting healthy ones in place, we need to enjoy the journey. So often we want to just get to the destination, and we miss the beauty of the scenery along the way. It will take a lifetime to journey to Jericho, so why not enjoy the ride?

Having the heart of a warrior means to commit to battle for good. Remember that God will be with us wherever we go: "Have I not commanded you? Be strong and courageous. Do not be afraid; do not be discouraged, for the LORD your God will be with you wherever you go" (Joshua 1:9).

Joshua was commissioned by God to not be afraid or discouraged. He told Joshua that He would be with him wherever he goes. This is true for us today. God will be with us wherever we go! Joshua obeyed God and followed His instruction. Joshua ordered the Israelites to march around the walls of Jericho, just as God had instructed—and they did. Joshua feared God in a Holy, reverential (healthy) way and moved forward in trust. "When the trumpets sounded, the army shouted, and at the sound of the trumpet, when the men gave a loud shout, the wall collapsed; so everyone charged straight in, and they took the city" (Joshua 6:20).

Just as Joshua followed the instructions of God and the walls of Jericho came crashing down, so will the walls of our hearts, if we are obedient. We need to confront our fears and then take action! We are all afraid, but we must press on. "Not confronting our fear denies the grace of God, and insults both His giving of the gift and His grace to sustain us as we are learning."—Henry Cloud, *Boundaries*. It doesn't matter how we start, it matters how we finish. Let's start knocking down those walls, and not lose heart.

Bob Wieland is a Vietnam veteran who lost his legs in an explosion in 1969. After recovering from his injuries, he was inspired to become a marathon participant. Over his lifetime he has finished many marathons, often taking multiple days to finish. He is the only double amputee to finish the difficult Kona, Hawaii, Ironman race without a wheelchair. He "ran" across America on his hands, taking three years, eight months, and six days to travel from coast to coast. Bob states, "I lost my legs, but I didn't lose my heart, and that's why I fell in love with New York," he said. "A lot of people have legs, but too many people have lost their hearts."

Dear sister, too many of us lose our hearts in the race of life. I encourage you not to lose heart. In fact, Warrior, I commission you to listen to God, to follow His commands, to not be afraid or discouraged, and to march and shout at those walls until they collapse. Then go in and take the city of your heart. You are a mighty Warrior, hand crafted by God to take on any battle that He sends you into.

We are more than conquers! Always reply with a "yes" to His invitation and fight the good fight. May your heart be one that is after God's own heart and not imprisoned by walls.

Jericho Girls' Response: Can you identify with them?

- *I now recognize that knowing and doing are two different things. I will practice the doing part more.*

- *Helping others helps me to bring down my walls.*

- *In difficult times and situations, I need to remember that many of my battles are spiritual.*

Jericho Girls' Tool Box:

Use your **welding torch** to mend and illuminate your heart.

"In the same way, let your light shine before others, that they may see your good deeds and glorify your Father in heaven" (Matthew 5:16).

Training Your Soul and Breaking Down Walls:

Dedicate the rest of your life to bringing down the walls of your heart that keep love out. You are loved!

EPILOGUE

There I was—back in the garden where it all began. I was different. Changed for the better, and awaiting God's next mission. I was hoping to hear something from God, "Well done good and faithful servant," or, "Good job bringing down those walls." But nothing—so I sat in silence. What did I expect? A pat on the back? Really? As I waited in hopes of hearing something, anything, a slight breeze enveloped me. I watched a squirrel scramble down a tree and a butterfly flutter past. Even though I was deep into the garden, I could still hear the traffic noise blocks away. The world was noisy and busy, but for the moment I was still and attentive to His whisper. I reflected on my journey to Jericho. So much had happened over the last year.

When I first met God in this garden a year ago, He informed me that I had walls to deal with. To my surprise, I found those walls hidden in the ancient city of my heart. My journey to Jericho went well— I thought—but I still needed affirmation from Him. I explored the inner depths of my heart by meeting with godly women.

During my year's journey I found that I indeed had walls—walls with others, but even more important, walls with God. I had built walls with God, because I was fearful of what God might ask of me. I was worried that He would have me do something I was not (in my mind) able to do. And He did. But what I began to see was that I was more than capable, just afraid to take the first step.

Not only did He have me identify, and break down my walls, He also stirred a desire in me to write about my experiences. I felt I was being led out of my comfort zone. But that is exactly what God calls us to do; crawl out of our comfort zones, and let our hearts beat fast, maybe even race a little. He calls us to live with excitement and passion.

Sharing my experience with others, letting them know my thoughts, made my heart race. It definitely took me out of my comfort zone and to a different level of trust. At first, I journalled and created lesson plans. As my journey progressed, it transformed into a book. God takes us to greater places than we can ever expect to go.

After identifying the types of walls I had, I began to identify who I truly am; one who is creative like my Creator. One who is serious at times and now likes that part of me. One who needs to live in relationship with others, and cannot do life alone. One who absolutely adores her husband, and loves every heartbeat with him. As I began to break down my walls, and discover who I truly am, I had a new love of self. I began to live in the moment, being present to those whom I was with. I learned to love life living outside my comfort zone and familiarity.

The Jericho Girls helped to affirm who I am, and most importantly, God did too. He created me uniquely, and I love His works. They are wonderful! Knowing who I am helped me to identify why I put up walls in the first place. We cannot possibly start anywhere else but with who we are. We need to embrace the fact that God made us a certain way for a certain purpose. That purpose is unique to each of us.

Getting real with God was a pivotal time for me, because if I cannot be real with God, who can I truly be real with? And who was I fooling anyway? He already knows the real me. I addressed my greatest struggles with Him—faith, trust, and control.

Trust was easier for me than faith and control. Faith was difficult for me, because even though He had worked out the intricate details of my life in the past, there were (and will be) times when I wasn't able to see what He was doing in the present. When things aren't going according to my plan, I tended towards (and still tend towards), losing perspective of my faith and what He will do with my future. Control was (and still is), difficult for me. Running ahead of God continues to get the best of me. I run ahead, but He continues to stay put until I return. He allows me to get back in step with Him.

Trust is easier for me because really, what other choice do I have but to trust Him? In John 6:25–59, Jesus delivers a difficult teaching. "Upon hearing it, many of His disciples said, 'This is a hard teaching. Who can accept it?' " (verse 60). Then Jesus asked in verse 67, "You do not want to leave me too, do you?" My favorite disciple, Peter, bursts forth and says in verses 68 and 69, "Lord, to Whom shall we go? You have the words of eternal life. We believe and know that you are the Holy One of God." I, like Peter, know this to be true in my heart. So I trust. Because, to whom shall I go, if not to Jesus? I also found comfort in reading about other people in the Bible who struggled with control issues, like me.

Getting real with the Jericho Girls helped me to reach out and ask for help. This newer form of transparency helped me connect on a deeper level with them.

Addressing walls of hurt was a pivotal moment, because it helped me to see things in a new light. Love is risky. God has the same risk factor with us—when we reject Him, He gets hurt. But He still gives us the opportunity to accept or reject Him. This then, is the true picture of love, which tells me that loving others and opening up is worth the risk of being hurt. True love never fails.

I discovered how to, in my own way, dance without a care without worrying about what others think. I evolved into a new spirit as I got the correct perspective on esteem. I have always loved who I am, as best as one can, but now it is different. I love who I am from God's goal perspective. Being true to whom I am and my beliefs has helped me to appreciate myself in a new and healthy way.

I began to be less inhibited, asking for help sooner, when needed. I began to be a better listener and not attempt to have all the answers and simply "fix" things for others. I built walls of promise around my heart to help protect it. I was transforming into the new and improved me and loving it!

As walls came crumbling down, I realized that fear is the root of the walls I build. When I fear, I build false walls to protect myself. But facing the fear, leaning into it, helps me to combat the problem. I came to the realization that God not only calls me to identify my fears, but He also expects me to face them so I do not live in fear. As I fought walls of resentment and bitterness, a new spirit emerged, that of a warrior ready to fight to keep those walls down. Love began to overtake my heart instead of resentment. I embarked on building healthy walls around my heart: walls of promise, correct self-esteem, correct self-talk, forgiveness, and love. I began to see things through God's perspective, acknowledging physical and spiritual battles. I am now dressed in the armor of God and ready to fight the life-long battle of keeping walls down and only allowing healthy ones to exist.

I heard a frog jump off a lily pad and when I looked up, I realized just how much time had passed. I recognized I didn't need to hear from Him that day or have Him show me a sign. I felt an unexplainable peace from within. It was Him. I could almost sense Him smiling. It was a great journey to Jericho.

A new and improved me had emerged and I felt a deeper love of self. Not self-absorbed, but almost as God would see me. I still have a long journey ahead of me. I will need to continually work on my walls while I am on this side of Heaven. But I am at peace about that, and it no longer seems the formidable task with God beside me.

My journey began in a garden, but it didn't end there. As I left the garden that day, I passed a lagoon area with dark, algae-filled water. The murky water was all I could focus on until I saw it; the reflection of the huge trees in the water. Their reflection was immensely beautiful in the water, but I almost missed it because I was staring at the muck.

I think we get stuck peering at the muck of our hearts, when all God sees is the beautiful reflection. I still have walls. Walls I have not even addressed yet. Walls that were not part of our year's journey of discussions. Many have come down and many more shall follow, but I am now better equipped to deal with them.

I left the garden smiling because I could now see the reflection of my heart. My heart was not hidden behind as many walls as before, and I was more transparent. As I left the lagoon area and headed out of the garden, I reflected on the scripture I read when I first came here:

> *Are you tired? Worn out? Burned out on religion? Come to me. Get away with me and you'll recover your life. I'll show you how to take a real rest. Walk with me and work with me—watch how I do it. Learn the unforced rhythms of grace. I won't lay anything heavy or ill-fitting on you. Keep company with me and you'll learn to live freely and lightly* (Matthew 11:28–30 MSG).

I believe I learned these "unforced rhythms of grace." I no longer knowingly build walls around my heart to protect it. God does not want us to have unnatural, ill-fitting confines. He calls us to live in this incredible rhythm with Him—a dance of love that is a bit risky but alive and revealing my heart in a new way. I am a warrior who is ready to fight to be who He has created me to be. I know Whose I am, and Who will lead me into the future battles of my heart. I will be fighting with you. Remember, that you are well equipped as you fight the good fight, and finish the race, and you are certainly not alone.

Love,

Your Sister Warrior

WALLS
of a WARRIOR
STUDY GUIDE
Leading a Jericho Girls Group

DAWNA HETZLER

And the Walls of Jericho came crashing down......

"When the trumpets sounded, the army shouted, and at the sound of the trumpet, when the men gave a loud shout, the wall collapsed; so everyone charged straight in, and they took the city" (Joshua 6:20 NIV).

Contents

Dear Leader,

You are about to embark on an incredible journey with God. As you lead your group, it is my prayer that you will be filled with wonderment while watching lives change and transform. This is a deep and personal journey for each person who participates.

When I founded the Jericho Girls group, I had no idea how intensely and profoundly it would change each of us. I believe God did not reveal the extent of the lessons we learned or the level of deep desires for our hearts to be free. If He had, I would have been too overwhelmed to sign up for the task. Upon reflection, I see that God moved in a mighty way in each of our lives. Know that He will move in yours too.

Recognize that everyone is at different levels of trust in their relationships. Take time to wait on God within the group, and during one-on-one discussions. Listen for wisdom, allowing God to guide and lead. It is in this place that the Holy Spirit moves others to share. There have been many lesson plans that I did not get through, simply because I allowed God to lead the conversation.

In Luke 5:1-11, Jesus was teaching a crowd of people on the shore while he sat in a boat close to the shoreline. When Jesus finished speaking to the people, He instructed Peter to "Put out into deep water, and let down the nets for a catch." Peter argued with Jesus that they had been fishing all night with no luck, but then he did as Jesus instructed him. Scripture tells us that the catch was so great, that their nets began to break. Peter had to signal to his partners in another boat to come and help. Peter recognized that this was a miracle from God. I believe this ministry is also a miracle from God. There is no other explanation, other than God, for the profound changes that occur when bringing down the walls of our hearts. Like Peter, you too can expect to have a "miraculous catch" by simply listening to God, as you lead.

Upon witnessing this miracle, Peter falls at Jesus' knees and proclaims, "Go away from me Lord; I am a sinful man." Sometimes we believe that we are not capable of leading. We can think that we're not worthy to lead, do not have enough education, are not wise enough, don't know the Bible well enough…. But look at what Jesus says to Peter: "Do not be afraid; from now on you will catch men." Jesus calls the unbelieving, the uneducated, the sinful person. He calls us to simply follow Him. Don't get caught up in the lie that you are unable to lead. By the mere fact that you are here, God is moving you to the front line. Believe in yourself!

Finally, in verse eleven it says, "So they pulled their boats up on shore, left everything, and followed Him." My hope is that each leader will passionately help others break down barriers, and build meaningful, transparent relationships with one another. I pray that you will be so moved by God's work within you, and your group, that you will have the same feeling as the disciples did: that you would leave **everything** and follow Him.

As you journey to Jericho and embark on breaking down walls of the heart, understand that there is a commitment involved. It is not always easy, it can be difficult. Change can be frightening. But doesn't God call us to grow? In Mark 1:16-17, Jesus called his disciples, Simeon Peter and Andrew, saying, "Come, follow me, and I will make you fishers of men." Go and become great fishers of men (and women). Follow Him, breaking down walls of the heart, that will forever change your life and others! May you never be the same.

Forming a Jericho Girls Group

What is a Jericho Girls group?

A Jericho Girls group is a group of women who meet at a particular location, to discuss the walls that they build around their hearts. Some groups meet weekly, some meet monthly.

Purpose: The purpose of the Jericho Girls' meetings is for women to improve their self-love, relationship with God, and others. At each meeting, the Jericho Girls use *Walls of a Warrior* and the study guide to better understand themselves, appreciate and love themselves more (as God loves them), build confidence, fear less, and develop healthy walls of the heart. The Jericho Girls will also work to develop deeper, transparent relationships with other women so that they can experience life *together*. These discoveries, when implemented, should then overflow into every relationship in their lives.

How do I form a Jericho Girls group? To begin a Jericho Girls group, first go to www.jerichogirls.com and register your group. Go to the Events tab, select Jericho Girls Group, and register your group there. You will be asked to sign the statement of faith. Once your group is registered, you will receive a confirmation email and your group will be posted on the Jericho Girls website.

What if I have questions or need support? You can send an email to jerichogirls@gmail.com and a team member will attend to your questions. Founder of The Jericho Girls Group, Dawna Hetzler, has a vision of connecting women worldwide. Her passion is for women to live closely to God, strengthen themselves, and love others well. It is our goal to make each individual Jericho Girls group a success. When the groups are successful, lives are transformed.

Jericho Girls' Group Guidelines

1. A Safe Environment

- The Jericho Girls' Group is a safe place for everyone. This means that each individual will be received and honored. The Jericho Girls is a place where hearts are shared, and that is a vulnerable place.

- There is no pressure to take part in discussions. If you need to just listen, that is alright. The group is about a commitment to share and to go deeper, but we will meet you where you are.

2. Confidentiality

- What is shared within the group, stays in the group.

- There will be no discussions with any persons within the group or outside of the group that would compromise someone's confidence. For example, If Jane shared a story within the group, Mary and Lisa cannot discuss Jane's story at any time! Lisa can discuss Jane's story only with Jane directly, and that is it. Confidentiality is essential.

3. No Judgement

- It is the responsibility of each Jericho Girl to maintain a safe, nonjudgmental environment. This means no snap answers. We are called to respect one another and listen well.

- During group discussions, try not to give advice. No quick fixes. Listening is of the utmost importance.

4. Transparency

- We will be transparent with one another. The goal of our gatherings is to break down walls of the heart. Each woman is expected to work on being open and honest to the best of her ability.

- No faking. Be real in your discussions.

5. Different Journeys

- Understand that every person's walk is not the same. We are all at different levels of faith, and are at different places in our life journey. Each experience is unique. Remember that each woman will share and open up at her own pace. Some need time to build trust. We will be patient and loving to all.

6. Pray

- We will commit to pray regularly for one another.

7. Committed

- We will be committed. Make a commitment to attend each meeting. Sign the Jericho Girls Commitment Contract. We understand that life gets busy and things happen, so do not feel guilty if you miss a meeting. However, when we break down walls together, it requires a commitment to yourself, and to the other women in the group.

8. Expectation

- Expect to see wonderful things happen, as we "do life" together and crush walls. As walls come crumbling down, you will discover Grace.

Meeting Details

Jericho Girls groups are designed for a two hour meeting time. More than that seems to be too overwhelming. Adjust times as you see fit.

1. Each chapter is to be read prior to attending the session.

2. Begin the session with prayer. This might seem like a no-brainer, but sometimes it is overlooked or forgotten.

3. Discuss the previous *Training your Soul.* Ask questions such as: What did the training do for you? What did you learn? What did you experience while training? How did it make you more like Jesus?

4. Read the given scripture.

5. Begin the group discussion questions. Discuss the chapter and given questions. Feel free to add your own questions.

6. Break into groups of two, for one-on-one discussion.

   • This is the secret ingredient to breaking down walls. Most of our wall deconstruction happens in this time together.

   • The leader will name the groups of twos. The groups should be different for each meeting. This gives each woman the opportunity to move out of their comfort zones, and share with a new person each time. This is an important time to be sensitive to the Holy Spirit about who should and should not be paired up. If you prefer, you can draw names.

   • Allow twenty to thirty minutes of one-on-one time. Each individual dedicates half of the time to answering, and discussing the proposed questions. Then the other partner is allowed to share for the remainder of the time.

7. When one-on-one time is complete, the group reconvenes. Next, share amongst the group what was learned from the one-on-one time. Final discussions are wrapped up.

8. Discuss the next Training Your Soul and Breaking Down Walls exercise and review Tool Box note cards.

9. End in prayer.

A time outline: Please adjust accordingly to fit the needs of your group.

Begin your meeting;

Fifteen Minutes: Opening prayer and discussion of training your soul and breaking down walls.

Note for the first meeting: Because there is no previous soul training, spend this time discussing the introduction.

Thirty to Forty Five Minutes: Read the given scripture, discuss the chapter, and the group questions.

Twenty to Thirty Minutes: Break into one-on-one groups for discussion.

Thirty Minutes: The last thirty minutes of the session, resume to group discussion and share what you learned from your one-on-one time. Remind the group to read the next chapter before the next meeting. Go over the upcoming Training Your Soul And Breaking Down Walls exercise. Review Tool Box note cards. End in prayer.

Definitions

Tool Box: The note cards are designed to remind each Jericho Girl of the tools it takes to build healthy walls. Memorize them if you can.

Training Your Soul And Breaking Down Walls:

When we train our souls, we are practicing spiritual disciplines. Spiritual disciplines are defined by Wikipedia.com as: *A spiritual practice or spiritual discipline (often including spiritual exercises) is the regular or full-time performance of actions and activities undertaken for the purpose of cultivating spiritual development. Therefore, a spiritual practice moves a person along a path towards a goal. The goal is variously referred to as salvation, liberation, or union (with God).*

As we train our souls and practice different spiritual disciplines, the goal is to become more like Jesus.

Jericho Girls' *Commitment Contract*

1. I commit to attending each meeting and to do my very best not to miss more than two sessions. Attendance is important to establish a level of trust within the group.

2. I make a commitment to grow spiritually with God, and with other women in the group. I will be transparent and commit to break down my heart walls.

3. I commit to reading each chapter before the next session.

4. I will practice the *training your soul and breaking down walls* spiritual disciplines.

5. I will create a safe environment for every woman. I will honor the words that are shared within the group and keep confidentiality.

6. I commit to pray for each woman within my group.

7. I will be honest with myself and my feelings. I will work to be God's warrior.

_____   _____

Jericho Girl   Date

Chapter 1

What Walls?

"By faith the walls of Jericho fell, after the people had marched around them for seven days" (Hebrews 11:30, NIV).

INTRODUCTIONS OF ATTENDEES

PRAYER

A BRIEF DISCUSSION OF GUIDELINES.

GROUP DISCUSSION:

GIVE A VERY BRIEF OVERVIEW FROM ABRAHAM TO MOSES.

READ:

Deuteronomy 34:5-12 and Joshua 1. Elaborate on the details of Joshua taking Moses' place as leader.

DISCUSS THE BOOK'S INTRODUCTION AND CHAPTER ONE.

Ask the group: What fears might someone have that would create walls? Make a list.

1. What types of walls can I identify with (structural walls, non-structural, floating walls, firewalls)? What walls do I have that I am aware of today?

2. Do I have walls with God? Identify. Discuss shame and fear.

<u>Shame:</u> the painful feeling arising from the consciousness of something dishonorable, improper, ridiculous, etc. done by one-self or another.

<u>Fear:</u> a distressing emotion aroused by impending danger, evil, pain, etc. whether the threat is real or imagined, the feeling or condition of being afraid.

<u>Vulnerability:</u> capable of or susceptible to being wounded or hurt; open to moral attack, criticism, temptation

3. What walls do I have with others? Discuss vulnerability.

*Time alone with God: Each Jericho Girl will find an area by herself and spend about 10 minutes alone with God. Ask God: What walls do I need to work on most in my life?

_____

_____

_____

_____

ONE-ON-ONE DISCUSSION: DISCUSS WITH YOUR PARTNER WHAT WALLS YOU HAVE.

WRAP UP DISCUSSION WITH THE GROUP:

What walls did you discover? Share if you are able.

JERICHO GIRLS' TOOL BOX:

Put on your *safety goggles* so your vision is not compromised.

"See, I have engraved you on the palms of my hands; your walls are ever before me" (Isaiah 49:16).

TRAINING YOUR SOUL AND BREAKING DOWN WALLS:

Lectio Divina (Latin for divine reading). Traditionally, lectio divina has four separate steps: read, meditate, pray and contemplate. First, a passage of Scripture is read, and then its meaning is reflected upon. This is followed by prayer and contemplation on the Word of God. Slowly read Joshua 6 practicing lectio divina. Note which words or verses really stick with you. Once you have some words or verses that really resonate with you, reread them slowly and meditate on them. Pray about what is on your heart after reading these words or verses. Read them not as text but rather as a love letter from God. Contemplate what God is saying to you. Come ready to share your findings at the next meeting.

Chapter 2

Who Am I?

PRAYER

DISCUSS TRAINING YOUR SOUL AND BREAKING DOWN WALLS:

What where your highlights as you read Joshua 6 over the past month? What did God say to you? Share a scripture or word from Joshua.

Moses was preparing Joshua to replace him as the leader to the Israelites. God disqualified Moses from being the leader and entering the Promised Land because of Moses' disobedience.

Do you remember why God disqualified Moses from entering the Promised Land?

READ:

Numbers 20:1-12

Moses was denied entrance into the Promised Land because he disobeyed God (Numbers 20:1-12). The first time the Israelites needed water, the Lord told Moses to strike a large rock and water came forth (Exodus 17:1-7). The second time He told Moses to speak to the rock. But Moses was angry and yelled at the people and then struck the rock twice, and again water came out. So what was the problem?

1. Moses' action demonstrated a lack of trust in God.

2. Moses believed that a word alone would not suffice.

Words have power. In Genesis, God spoke things into being. Jesus spoke words and healings took place. God asked Moses to speak to the rock so that life-giving water would flow out of it.

As we speak life-giving words to each other about our walls, our walls will begin to break down. Our words also have the power to hurt. That is why trust is so vital. Since God can bring water from a rock by speaking to it, so can He also bring water (new life) to the walls around our hearts. Speaking about our walls and sharing with others, we will begin to see change. Do you believe that? God also used words/sounds to bring down the walls of Jericho.

Moses pleaded with God to go into the Promised Land (Deuteronomy 3:21 -29).

Have you pleaded with God only for Him to say no? Are you ok with God's answer and plan for your life?

Next we see Moses observing the Promised Land and the death of Moses (Deuteronomy 34).

God then begins to raise Joshua as a leader.

Review the main topics of Joshua 1-6.

GROUP DISCUSSION:

What did God tell Joshua three times in Joshua chapter 1? (See vses. 6, 7, and 9).

What stood out to you in Chapter 2, Walls of a Warrior?

- What defines who I am?
- "Others" define who I am? What are some of the "others"? parents, mistakes….? (How are your children being defined?)
- How does "the world" define who I am?
- Who does God say I am?
- What can we do to help remember who we are in Christ?
    - » Stay in God's word
    - » Practice what we learn in God's word

» Have relationships with Godly women – foster and nourish

» Spend time alone with God daily

» Prayer

Words matter. Other people's words can define who we are. Our theology about God that was taught to us (correct and incorrect teachings) can define who we are.

ONE-ON-ONE DISCUSSION:

1. Who am I? Tell your discussion partner your labels. Are you a mother, business person, spouse, single?

    _____

    _____

    _____

    _____

    _____

2. Who am I—*REALLY?* Close your eyes and think about who you are on the inside. Share with your partner who you truly are. How has God "hard wired" you? What are your likes and dislikes? What are the inner desires of your heart?

    _____

    _____

    _____

    _____

    _____

WRAP UP DISCUSSION WITH THE GROUP:

Walls of a Warrior informs us that the scriptures, as well as our friends, tell us who we are. Discuss.

Jericho Girls' Tool box:

Quit *hammering* on yourself!

"Therefore, if anyone is in Christ, he is a new creation; the old has gone, the new has come!" (2 Corinthians 5:17).

Training Your Soul And Breaking Down Walls:

When you write things, they become more real. Journal the things that characterize you, as who you really are. What do you enjoy? What makes you tick? Once you have made a list, study it and begin to embrace and love who you really are, because that's who God uniquely made you to be! Next, create a separate list of your attributes that are out of place in God's creation and that should be purged. Once you have made this list, review it and begin to disassociate from these attributes that do not define who you really are. Finally, look through the book of Psalms. Which one speaks to you about who you are? Pick a Psalm denoting where you are with God in your walk today and pray it daily.

Psalm 5: A Prayer for Guidance

Psalm 6: A Prayer of Faith in Time of Distress

Psalm 10: A Prayer of Confidence in God's triumph over Evil

Psalm 23: The Lord, the Shepherd of His People

Psalm 25: A plea for Deliverance and Forgiveness

Psalm 28: Rejoicing in Answered Prayer

Psalm 31: The Lord a Fortress in Adversity

Psalm 32: The Joy of Forgiveness

Psalm 34: The Happiness of those Who Trust in God

Psalm 35: The Lord the Avenger of His People

Psalm 38: Prayer in Time of Chastening

Psalm 39: Prayer for Wisdom and Forgiveness

Chapter 3

Getting Real With God

PRAYER

DISCUSS TRAINING YOUR SOUL AND BREAKING DOWN WALLS:

What did you discover about yourself writing down, *Who you are.* Did you discover any attributes that should be purged from your thinking?

GROUP DISCUSSION:

READ:

Deuteronomy 3:21-29

Moses pleaded with God to allow him to enter the Promised Land. Moses was *real* with God. Despite Moses' plea, God still said no to Moses.

1. Have you ever begged God for something only to have Him say no? How did that make you feel?

2. What do you think would happen if you told God what you really thought and felt?

3. Discuss your faith, trust, and control issues that you have with God. Which is the most difficult? Which is the easiest for you?

4. Read John 11:17-37. Have you ever had a BUT Mary moment in your life? Discuss.

One-On-One Discussion:

1. What are some of my issues, problems, troubles, or fears that I am holding on to? What does it look like to let God have control over them? Why is it difficult to *truly* discuss these with God?

2. What is keeping me from letting go of my issues, problems, troubles, and or fears? How can I get real with God about them?

3. What do you struggle with the most? Faith, Trust, or Control?

Wrap Up Discussion With The Group:

What did you find most helpful in your one-on-one discussion about getting real with God? Share so that the group can benefit from your findings.

Jericho Girls' Tool Box:

Let God *rule* your day!

"I will instruct you and teach you in the way you should go; I will counsel you and watch over you" (Psalm 32:8).

Training Your Soul And Breaking Down Walls:

Trust God throughout your day. Relinquish control to Him each day. Have faith in what God can do. You might have to do these things hourly, or even minute-by-minute.

Chapter 4

Getting Real With Others

DISCUSS TRAINING YOUR SOUL AND BREAKING DOWN WALLS:

How did you do? What did you learn about God? What did you learn about yourself during this practice? Trust God throughout your day. Relinquish control to Him each day. Have faith in what God can do. You might have to do these things hourly, or even minute by minute.

GROUP DISCUSSION:

- Your highlights from this chapter?

- Write down the name of a person you can be real with. Qualities?

READ:

Deuteronomy 31:6

1. Why is getting real with others such a tough topic?

2. Why is it difficult to ask for help? Discuss pride and why it can be so dangerous.

3. Appearance—Why is appearance so important to us?

4. What causes shame? Why is shame unhealthy?

5. Discuss false appearance. Have you tried to appear better than you actually are? Discuss.

6. Compare and contrast the Proverbs 31 woman to our world view of beauty today.

ONE-ON-ONE DISCUSSION:

1. Whose opinion is most important to you in your life right now? Whose opinion *should* be most important?

_____

_____

_____

2. How can I be more real with myself and others?

_____

_____

_____

a. Sharing my experiences in life:

_____

_____

_____

b. Quit worrying about my appearance:

_____

_____

_____

c. No longer carrying around shame:

_____

_____

_____

3. How would the way you live be different if you didn't depend on your performance to receive love from others?

_____

_____

_____

WRAP UP DISCUSSION WITH THE GROUP:

What "ah ha" moments did you glean from your one-on-one discussion?

JERICHO GIRLS' TOOL BOX:

Quit *wrenching* on yourself!

"I am fearfully and wonderfully made; your works are wonderful" (Psalm 139:14).

TRAINING YOUR SOUL AND BREAKING DOWN WALLS:

See yourself as God sees you—one who is worthy of His Love. Each time you are hard on yourself, remember that God delights in you! Spend some time in Psalm 139. Remind yourself that you are "fearfully and wonderfully made."

Chapter 5

Walls of Hurt

PRAYER

DISCUSS TRAINING YOUR SOUL AND BREAKING DOWN WALLS:

How did you do? What did you learn about God? What did you learn about yourself during this practice? See yourself as God sees you—one who is worthy of His Love. Each time you are hard on yourself, remember that God delights in you! Spend some time in Psalm 139. Remind yourself that you are "fearfully and wonderfully made."

READ:

I Samuel 20:12-17

II Samuel 4:4

II Samuel 9

II Samuel 19:24-30

GROUP DISCUSSION:

- How do you think Mephibosheth felt about David *before* meeting him? Describe some of his emotions.

- How do you think Mephibosheth felt *after* meeting David?

- How might you have felt in the same circumstances?

- How do you think David might have felt about Mephibosheth not coming with him?

- How do you think he sorted out who was telling the truth—Ziba or Mephibosheth?

- Did it matter if he sorted out the truth?

- What standard did David use to make his decisions?

- Have you been hurt? Share an experience?

- How do we tend to react when we have been hurt?

- What are some things we can do to heal our hurts?

1. Do you run and hide? Add more bricks to your hurt wall? Have a pity party, attempt to do life alone? Confront and attempt to resolve? OR???

2. Do you run towards God or away? Why do you think you run towards or away?

3. Have you been "dropped"? What do you do when you are "dropped"? Do you build walls?

4. Can you identify with Joseph regarding how he chose to forgive his brothers?

5. What *should* our response be to hurt?

ONE-ON-ONE DISCUSSION:

Say to your discussion partner: I have been hurt, but I refuse to hide behind my wall of hurt.

1. Write what the following means to you and discuss with your discussion partner.

   a: Love your enemies:

   _____

   _____

   b: Do good to those who hate you:

   _____

   _____

c. Bless those who curse you:

_____

_____

d. Pray for those who mistreat you:

_____

_____

2. Why is this so difficult for us to do?

WRAP UP DISCUSSION WITH THE GROUP:

How do we put these things we learned about hurt into practice?

JERICHO GIRLS' TOOL BOX:

Sister, *level* with yourself. Are hurts truly as bad as you think they are? If they are, can you decide to face them, forgive them, and move on?

"Weeping may endure for a night but joy comes in the morning" (Psalm 30:5).

TRAINING YOUR SOUL AND BREAKING DOWN WALLS:

Do a simple act of kindness for someone. Reach out to someone, say or do something kind. This can be a simple gesture; holding someone's hand or sharing a hug. Forgive someone who has deeply hurt you. Begin to pray for that person.

Chapter 6

Walls Of Esteem

PRAYER

DISCUSS TRAINING YOUR SOUL AND BREAKING DOWN WALLS:

How did you do? What did you learn about God? What did you learn about yourself during this practice? Do a simple act of kindness for someone. Reach out to someone, say or do something kind. This can be a simple gesture; holding someone's hand or sharing a hug. Forgive someone who has deeply hurt you. Begin to pray for that person.

READ:

2 Samuel 6:16-23

GROUP DISCUSSION:

1. Define what esteem means to you:

_____

_____

_____

Merriam-Webster.com defines it as, "The regard in which one is held; worth and value."

2. Do you regard yourself with worth and value? Do you respect and admire yourself? We can have a healthy self-image or an unhealthy self-image. There is a difference between the two.

3. What are your conceived imperfections? What do you dislike about yourself that potentially seems fine to another person?

4. Do you worry about what others think? To what degree?

5. Evaluate your self-talk. How does it need to improve?

6. Do you worship before the Lord without a care of what others think? Daily?

ONE-ON-ONE DISCUSSION:

1. Who do you relate to most in the story: with Uzzah, David, or Michal and why?

_____

_____

_____

2. Do you think you have a healthy self-image or an unhealthy one?

_____

_____

_____

3. What would make you dance before the Lord with all you're might without a care what others thought?

_____

_____

_____

WRAP UP DISCUSSION WITH THE GROUP:

How did you answer question 3?

JERICHO GIRLS' TOOL BOX:

Pencil in time to love who you are.

"Your beauty should not come from outward adornment, such as elaborate hairstyles and the wearing of gold jewelry or fine clothes.

Rather, it should be that of your inner self, the unfading beauty of a gentle and quiet spirit, which is of great worth in God's sight" (1 Peter 3:3–4).

Training Your Soul And Breaking Down Walls:

Evaluate your worship to God. Do you need to change the way you respond to God's love so that your worship is pure and reckless for Him? Do something that makes you dance before the Lord with all your might, without caring what others think about you.

Oscar Wilde said: "Be yourself; everyone else is already taken."

Chapter 7

Walls of Masks

DISCUSS TRAINING YOUR SOUL AND BREAKING DOWN WALLS:

How did you do? What did you learn about God? What did you learn about yourself during this practice? Evaluate your worship to God. Do you need to change the way you respond to God's love so that your worship is pure and reckless for Him? Do something that makes you dance before the Lord with all your might without caring what others think about you.

GROUP DISCUSSION:

READ:

Jesus wept.

He was never afraid of showing His emotions. He didn't put on a "tough guy" mask. Jesus wept over the death of Lazarus (John 11:35), He wept over Jerusalem (Luke 19:41), and Jesus wept tears of anguish in the garden. (Luke 22:39-46 and Hebrews 5:7)

Jesus clears the temple. He gets mad in the temple, showing his emotions. (John 2:12-22)

1. What masks do you wear?

_____

_____

_____

2. What does your mask do for you?

_____

_____

_____

3. Can you think of a time when wearing a mask allowed you to do something or say something that you might not have without it?

_____

_____

_____

_____

4. What do we hide behind?

_____

_____

_____

5. Have you worn a mask for a long time that you need to chisel off?

_____

_____

_____

6. Do you think you will be able to take the mask off quickly, or will it take time to remove? What is holding you back from getting that mask off quicker?

_____

_____

_____

ONE-ON-ONE DISCUSSION:

1. With your discussion partner, discuss a mask that you wear or that you have worn in the past. Share why you would like to keep or remove this mask.

2. Discuss the differences between worldly tolerance and Biblical tolerance.

3. Why do you think wearing a mask is displeasing to God?

"We understand how dangerous a mask can be. We all become what we pretend to be." Patrick Rothfuss, *The Name of the Wind*.

WRAP UP DISCUSSION WITH THE GROUP:

Jesus was real. How do we become more real, like Him, and quit wearing masks?

JERICHO GIRLS' TOOL BOX:

Chisel away those masks!

"Every word of God is flawless; He is a shield to those who take refuge in Him" (Proverbs 30:5).

TRAINING YOUR SOUL AND BREAKING DOWN WALLS:

Be aware of when you are wearing your mask(s) and when you are not. When you realize you are hiding behind a mask, ask God to be the only shield you need. Allow someone see a glimpse of the real you—I bet they will like what they see!

Chapter 8

Walls Of Isolation

PRAYER

DISCUSS TRAINING YOUR SOUL AND BREAKING DOWN WALLS:

How did you do? What did you learn about God? What did you learn about yourself during this practice? Be aware of when you are wearing your mask(s) and when you are not. When you realize you are hiding behind a mask, ask God to be the only shield you need. Allow someone see a glimpse of the real you—I bet they will like what they see!

GROUP DISCUSSION:

READ:

Joshua 5:13-15, 6:1-5, 6:6-14, 6:15-21

1. One of the major walls that blocks our spiritual vision, is a wall that guards us and hides us from God, and true Christian relationships. This is called a wall of isolation. Are you isolated right now? What has caused you to isolate yourself?

    _____

    _____

    _____

2. How do you envision eliminating that wall?

_____

_____

_____

3. How have you lost sight of God's promise(s) for your life? What wall of promise do you need to erect?

_____

_____

_____

4. Why is isolation one of the worst walls?

_____

_____

_____

5. Why does isolation make us "weary warriors"?

_____

_____

_____

ONE-ON-ONE DISCUSSION:

1. Who are your armed guards and your rear guards? Do you have a least two? How do they help you through life and point you back to God?

_____

_____

_____

2. Discuss if it is easier for you to isolate or reach out for help.

_____

_____

3. Tell your discussion partner how they can help you, so that you do not build a wall of isolation.

Wrap Up Discussion With The Group:

Write a note to God and answer the following questions:

What is the main, unhealthy wall that you hold tight to your heart that needs to come crumbling down right now?

What wall of promise do you need to erect around your heart?

Jericho Girls' Tool Box:

Let God be your *wrecking ball!*

"The LORD will fight for you; you need only to be still" (Exodus 14:14).

Training Your Soul And Breaking Down Walls:

Set up a meeting with each of your "armed guards"—both front and rear. Talk with them about how you envision them helping you facilitate your walk with God. Maybe you do not have front and rear guards and need some. Maybe you just need a front or a rear. If so, meet with these people and talk with them about being one of your bodyguards. Pray for your armed guards as they march through life with you.

"We mutually disclose information about ourselves on increasingly deeper levels if we want to develop an increasingly closer and more meaningful friendship." Pamela Hoover Heim-Women School of Ministry Leadership. From an article, *Avoiding Mouth Traps.*

Chapter 9

Stop, Drop, And Listen!

LISTENING GROUPS

PRAYER

DISCUSS TRAINING YOUR SOUL AND BREAKING DOWN WALLS:

How did you do? What did you learn about God? What did you learn about yourself during this practice? Set up a meeting with each of your "armed guards"—both front and rear. Talk with them about how you envision them helping you facilitate your walk with God. Maybe you do not have front and rear guards and need some. Maybe you just need a front or a rear. If so, meet with these people and talk with them about being one of your bodyguards. Pray for your armed guards as they march through life with you.

LISTENING GROUPS:

Break into groups of two.

- Silence (one minute)

- Speaker speaks for a given amount of time (ten minutes or more)

Listener prays while listening to the speaker. The listener cannot speak during this time. Listener can jot down some notes as needed (e.g., a word from God or something that the speaker says that strikes a chord).

- Silence (one minute)

- Speaker invites a response from the listener (five minutes)

Reverse roles, the speaker now becomes the listener.

- Silence
- Speaker speaks for a given amount of time

Listener prays while listening to the speaker. Listener can jot down some notes as needed (e.g., a word from God, something that the speaker says that strikes a chord).

- Silence
- Speaker invites a response

Wrap Up Discussion With The Group:

Return to the group and discuss what you learned about listening.

Jericho Girls' Tool Box:

Sand and smooth those walls that have come crumbling down.

"Be still and know that I am God" (Psalm 46:10).

Training Your Soul And Breaking Down Walls:

Practice "three-way" listening—you, the person speaking, and God. Incorporate praying while listening to the person speaking to you. Really hear that person, while listening for the still small voice, the whisper you know to be His. Push back your own thoughts and ideas and allow room for God's Word and wisdom to fill you, so that you are able to be used in a mighty way.

Chapter 10

Walls of Resentment and Fear

PRAYER

DISCUSS TRAINING YOUR SOUL AND BREAKING DOWN WALLS:

How did you do? What did you learn about God? Practice "three-way" listening—you, the person speaking, and God. Incorporate praying while listening to the person speaking to you. Really hear that person, while listening for the still small voice, the whisper you know to be His. Push back your own thoughts and ideas and allow room for God's Word and wisdom to fill you, so that you are able to be used in a mighty way.

GROUP DISCUSSION:

READ:

Mathew 14:22-33 and 2 Peter 1:3.

1. What causes resentment?

_____

_____

_____

2. Do you believe you have resentment in your heart? What has been said or done to you that has caused resentment?

_____

_____

_____

3. Why is it tough to identify and overcome resentment?

_____

_____

_____

4. As God's warriors, what are we called to do about resentment?

_____

_____

_____

5. What is the root of all of our walls?

_____

_____

_____

6. The author says, "If we only acknowledge our fears but we do nothing to overcome them, we are no better off." How do we overcome our fears?

_____

_____

_____

ONE-ON-ONE DISCUSSION:

1. The author has a friend who had a wall of resentment with her husband. Can you identify with that wall?

_____

_____

2. The thing I struggle most with in my relationships is:

_____

_____

3. Name the thing you would most like to change in your relationships:

_____

_____

WRAP UP DISCUSSION WITH THE GROUP:

What are the "kites and snakes" in your life?

JERICHO GIRLS' TOOL BOX:

Sledgehammer those walls!

"Be strong and courageous. Do not be afraid; do not be discouraged, for the Lord your God will be with you wherever you go" (Joshua 1:9).

TRAINING YOUR SOUL AND BREAKING DOWN WALLS:

Spend some time in prayer humbly asking God for the grace to see clearly what walls of fear, and/or resentment you might have. You might want to journal your feelings. When you discuss your resentments and fears before God, what emotions come to the surface? Bring these feelings to God and sit with them quietly before Him. Write down how He might have you deal with them.

Chapter 11

Healthy Walls

PRAYER

DISCUSS TRAINING YOUR SOUL AND BREAKING DOWN WALLS:

How did you do? What did you learn about God? What did you learn about yourself during this practice? Spend some time in prayer humbly asking God for the grace to see clearly what walls of fear, and/or resentment you might have. You might want to journal your feelings. When you discuss your resentments and fears before God, what emotions come to the surface? Bring these feelings to God and sit with them quietly before Him. Write down how He might have you deal with them.

GROUP DISCUSSION:

READ:

Joshua Chapter 2

1. Why am I so hard on myself? What am I hard on myself about?

    _____

    _____

    _____

2. What does forgiveness of myself look like?

    _____

    _____

3. What does comparison do? Makes us think of ourselves
    as_____ or _____ than others.

4. Why is this so dangerous?

_____

_____

_____

ONE-ON-ONE DISCUSSION:

1. What do I need to do to live beyond the unhealthy walls that I have known for so many years, and began to construct healthy ones?

_____

_____

_____

2. What is keeping me from opening up, bringing down the walls of my heart, and displaying a "rope" like Rahab, in the window of my heart? Are you able to ask for help?

_____

_____

_____

3. How do you own *whose* you are?

_____

_____

_____

Other notes:

_____

_____

_____

WRAP UP DISCUSSION WITH THE GROUP:

How do you plan to build healthy walls of forgiveness, promise, esteem, and love around your heart?

JERICHO GIRLS' TOOL BOX:

Quit trying to *measure* up to others.

"If anyone thinks they are something when they are not, they deceive themselves. Each one should test their own actions. Then they can take pride in themselves alone, without comparing themselves to someone else, for each one should carry their own load" (Galatians 6:3–5).

TRAINING YOUR SOUL AND BREAKING DOWN WALLS:

Spend a day focused on your inner beauty and not your external. Think about the gifts that God has given you. Can you go a whole day in public without wearing makeup? Can you wear something frumpy and still feel beautiful? What do you need to give up in order to remind yourself how beautiful you are without those "things"? Decide what that is and then spend a whole day going without that thing, and meditating on the beautiful you—without comparing yourself to others.

Chapter 12

Ready for Battle

PRAYER

DISCUSS TRAINING YOUR SOUL AND BREAKING DOWN WALLS:

How did you do? What did you learn about God? What did you learn about yourself during this practice? Spend a day focused on your inner beauty and not your external. Think about the gifts that God has given you. Can you go a whole day in public without wearing makeup? Can you wear something frumpy and still feel beautiful? What do you need to give up in order to remind yourself how beautiful you are without those "things"? Decide what that is and then spend a whole day going without that thing and meditating on the beautiful you—without comparing yourself to others.

GROUP DISCUSSION:

READ:

Ephesians 6:10-12

1. What battles do you face right now in your life?

    _____

    _____

    _____

2. Why is the armor of God so important?

    _____

    _____

3. What "piece of armor" do you see yourself lacking?

_____

_____

4. Why are we victorious in community and not on or own?

_____

_____

_____

5. What does it look like to continue to bring down unhealthy walls and fight to maintain healthy walls?

_____

_____

_____

ONE-ON-ONE DISCUSSION:

1. Why is knowing different than doing? How do I move from knowing to doing?

_____

_____

_____

2. Where do I go from here?

_____

_____

_____

3. Ask your sister for help, right this moment. Complete this statement: "I need help with _____ right now in my walk with God. Will you help me break down this wall, and walk with me, sister-warrior?

"I can do all things through Christ who strengthens me" (Philippians 4:13 NIV).

Wrap Up Discussion With The Group:

The final commission: Dear sister, too many of us lose our hearts in the race of life. I encourage you not to lose heart. In fact, Warrior, I commission you to listen to God, to follow His commands, to be fearless and confident, and to march and shout at those walls until they collapse. Then go in and take the city of your heart. You are a mighty Warrior, hand crafted and equipped by God to take on any battle that He sends you into.

We are more than conquers! Always reply with a "yes" to His invitation and fight the good fight. May your heart be one that is after God's own heart and not imprisoned by walls.

Jericho Girls' Tool Box:

Use your *welding torch* to mend and illuminate your heart.

"In the same way, let your light shine before others, that they may see your good deeds and glorify your Father in heaven" (Matthew 5:16).

Training Your Soul And Breaking Down Walls:

Dedicate the rest of your life to bringing down the walls of your heart that keep love out. You are loved!

Put on your safety goggles
so your vision is not compromised

See, I have engraved you
on the palms of my hands
your walls are ever before me.

Isaiah 49:16

Quit hammering on yourself!

Therefore, if anyone is in
Christ, she is a new
creation; the old has gone,
the new has come!

— 2 Corinthians 5:17

Let God rule your day!

I will instruct you and
teach you in the way
you should go;
I will counsel you and
watch over you.

Psalm 32:8

Quit wrenching on yourself!

I am fearfully and
wonderfully made,
your works are wonderful!

Psalm 139:14

Sister, level with yourself!
Are your hurts truly that bad?
Can you decide to move on?

Weeping may endure for a
night but joy comes
in the morning!
Psalm 30:5

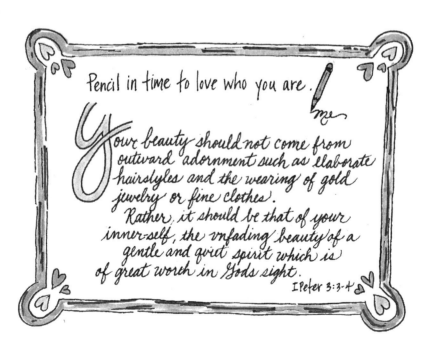

Pencil in time to love who you are.
me

Your beauty should not come from
outward adornment such as elaborate
hairstyles and the wearing of gold
jewelry or fine clothes.
Rather, it should be that of your
inner-self, the unfading beauty of a
gentle and quiet spirit which is
of great worth in God's sight.
I Peter 3:3-4

chisel away those masks!

Every word of God is flawless;
He is a shield to
those who take refuge in Him.
♥ Proverbs 30:5

Let God be your wrecking ball!

The LORD will fight for you;
you need only to be still.

Exodus 14:14

Quit trying to measure up to others.

If anyone thinks they are something when they are not they decieve themselves. Each one should test their own actions. Then they can take pride in themselves alone, without comparing themselves to someone else, for each one should carry their own load. Galatians 6:3-5

use your welding torch to mend and illuminate your heart...

In the same way let your light shine before others, that they may see your good deeds and glorify your father in heaven. Matthew 5:16

WORKS CITED

Barton, Ruth Haley. Sacred Rhythms. Downers Grove: Inter Varsity Press, 2006.

Card, Michael. A Fragile Stone. Downers Grove: Inter Varsity Press, 2003.

Cloud, Henry. Boundaries. Grand Rapids: Zondervan, 1992.

Coan, Robert Emery and Jim. "What causes chest pain when feelings are hurt?" Scientific American, February 2010.

DR SUSAN HYATT, DR EDDIE HYATT, VALARIE OWEN. God's Word to Women. n.d. http://godswordtowomen.org/help.htm.

Griffin, Emilie. Small Surrenders. Brewster: Paraclete Press, 2007.

Heim, Pamela Hoover. "Avoiding Mouth Traps." n.d.

The Breakfast Club. Directed by John Huges. 1985.

Lewis, C.S. The Screwtape Letters. HarperOne, 1942.

Lucado, Max. Cure for the Common Life. Nashville: W Publishing Group, 2005.

Mains, Karen. "The Healing Power of Being Deeply Heard." White Papers on Listening Growth Groups, West Chicago, IL, 2011.

Meberg, Marilyn. Devotionals Daily, The Shame Monster. March 18, 2013. http://devotionalsdaily.com/the-shame-monster/ (accessed 2013).

Millard, Bart. The Story Behind The Song (n.d.).

Miller, Lauren, interview by Colorado's Best TV Program. (2012).

Rosenau, Jeff. When Christians Act Like Christians. Centennial: Accountability Ministries, 2010.

Rothfuss, Patrick. Goodreads. n.d. http://www.goodreads.com/quotes/348276-we-understand-how-dangerous-a-mask-can-be-we-all (accessed 2013).

Scazzero, Geri. I Quit! Grand Rapids: Zondervan, 2010.

Smith, James Bryan. The Good and Beautiful God. Downers Grove: Inter Varsity Press, 2009.

Your Move. Performed by Andy Stanley. n.d.

The Vow. Directed by Michael Sucsy. 2012.

The Help. Directed by Tate Taylor. 2011.

UNGRADY, DAVE. "25 Years Later, a Marathon Finish Still Inspires." New York Times, 2011.

Voskamp, Ann. A Holy Experience. n.d. http://www.aholyexperience.com/2013/04/40-things-you-need-to-know-before-your-40-letters-to-a-woman-mid-way/.

Young, Sara. Jesus Calling. Nashville: Thomas Nelson, 2004.

ABOUT THE AUTHOR

DAWNA HETZLER is an award-winning author, national speaker, and Bible study teacher.

Dawna founded a women's group called, the "Jericho Girls" where women meet to discuss the walls they build around their hearts. After forming the group, Dawna realized that she too had walls. She began to write about her journey with the Jericho Girls. This journal inspired her to write her book, *Walls of a Warrior*. It's Dawna's vision that reading about her journey will inspire women to begin their own Jericho Girls groups and break down walls of hearts worldwide.

Dawna was born and raised in Southern California. In 1989 she married her high school sweetheart, David, and eventually moved to Colorado in 1993. Currently, she resides in Colorado with her two rescue Siberian Huskies. Dawna is the broker and owner of her own real estate firm, New Dawn Realty.

Dawna is not a morning person and need lots of coffee to get her moving, thinking and possibly even breathing. She enjoys golf, motorcycle riding with her husband, preparing lesson plans for her Bible study group, and simply spending time with her 'sister-girls'. For more information, visit her website at: DawnaHetzler.com.

① What do u think the solution is?

② what do u hear God calling you to do?

③ What do you need to lay down at the feet of Jesus? And are you able to do that?

Repeat James 1:19 when angry.

CPSIA information can be obtained
at www.ICGtesting.com
Printed in the USA
FSOW02n0902280915
11613FS

9 781937 801533